Zarpazo

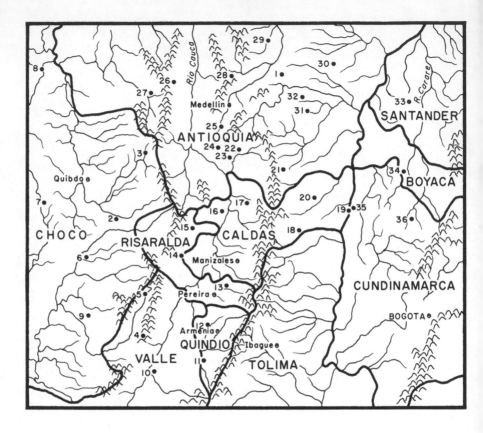

1. Sto. Domingo	13. Sta. Rosa	25. Caldas
2. Bagado	14. Apia	26. Caicedo
3. El Carmen	15. Mistrato	27. Urrao
4. El Dovio	16. Supia	28. San Pedro
5. El Cairo	17. Pacora	29. Carolina
6. Condoto	18. Marquetalia	30. Maceo
7. Alto Baudo (Pie de Pato)	19. La Dorada	31. San Carlos
	20. Samana	32. San Rafael
8. Bojaya	21. Argelia	33. San Fernando
9. Sipi	22. Montebella	34. Otanche
10. Bugalagrande	23. Santa Barbara	35. Puerto Salgar
11. Genova	24. Fredonia	36. La Palma
12. Montenegro		

Zarpazo
The Bandit

MEMOIRS OF AN UNDERCOVER

AGENT OF THE COLOMBIAN ARMY

EVELIO BUITRAGO SALAZAR

SERGEANT 2ND CLASS (RET.)

Translated by
M. MURRAY LASLEY

Edited, with an Introduction and
Explanatory Notes by
RUSSELL W. RAMSEY

THE UNIVERSITY OF ALABAMA PRESS
University, Alabama

The publisher wishes to acknowledge the assistance of the Office for International Studies and Programs of The University of Alabama in the preparation and financing of this volume.

Library of Congress Cataloging in Publication Data

Buitrago Salazar, Evelio.
    Zarpazo the bandit.

    Translation of Zarpazo.
    SUMMARY: The experiences of an army intelligence operative who specialized in penetrating bandit gangs during "*la violencia*," a series of internal wars in Colombia from 1946–1965.
    1. Colombia—History—1946– 2. Buitrago Salazar, Evelio. 3. Zarpazo, d. 1967. 4. Brigands and robbers—Colombia. [1. Colombia—History—1946– 2. Buitrago Salazar, Evelio. 3. Zarpazo, d. 1967. 4. Robbers and outlaws—Colombia] I. Title.
F2278.B813   986.1'063   76–10678
ISBN 0-8173-5600-2

Translated into English from
"*Zarpazo*": *Otra Cara de la Violencia/Memorias de un Suboficial del Ejército de Colombia* (Bogotá: Ministry of Defense, 1968).

Contents

Editor's Introduction

SERGEANT BUITRAGO
AND *LA VIOLENCIA*

Evelio Buitrago Salazar was a career enlisted man in the Colombian Army. The adventures he relates in *Zarpazo* provide an important window into several regions and periods of modern Colombia's greatest national tragedy—*la violencia*—the largest war in the Western hemisphere since the Mexican Revolution of 1910. *La violencia* consisted of a series of internal conflicts that beset Colombia from August, 1946, until June, 1965. Barely touching the cities, the struggle took place primarily in the interior highlands, with one large episode in the *llanos orientales. La violencia*, based upon traditional internal rivalries, took about one hundred sixty thousand lives and inflicted incredible economic and psychological damage on the nation. In all its cultural and political dimensions *la violencia* was one of the most complex domestic struggles in the twentieth century. The movement can be understood only as it relates to the rich and violent background of the Colombian nation, and especially to the *mestizo* culture of the interior highlands where the conflict was centered.

Although they did not leave any monumental structures such as those of the Inca or Maya civilizations, the Chibcha who occupied the highland plateau of Colombia were remarkable in many ways. Calling themselves the *Muiscas*, they developed intensive agriculture and an elaborate societal structure. The Chibcha were also fierce fighters, perfecting advanced patterns of warfare. Their artistic work and their practice of adorning their chieftain in gold dust fascinated Spanish adventurers and created the legend of El Dorado. In

1538 Gonzalo Jiménez de Quesada seized the Chibcha region and founded the city of Santa Fe de Bogotá. Although fighting continued for several decades, the Indians were eventually subdued and parceled out to their conquerors. The Spanish and Indians were fused in blood and culture, producing an authentic *mestizo* race. The land provided sufficient food to allow some leisure and the climate led to vigorous outdoor social habits, all part of an isolated, unexciting agrarian and pastoral society. Great haciendas were administered by wealthy Creole families. Churches, monasteries, and governmental buildings were constructed in the principal towns, providing outstanding examples of rich baroque architecture. Despite its isolation, Bogotá enjoyed prestige as the leading political and religious center, becoming a viceroyalty in 1717.

New Grenada remained stable and peaceful throughout most of the seventeenth and eighteenth centuries. In 1781, however, when royal officials enforced unpopular taxation measures, revolts broke out in the northern sectors of the viceroyalty. Known as the Comunero Revolt, the rebellion spread southward, involving some 6,000 men by April, 1781. Lacking cohesion and leadership, the movement was soon crushed, but it reflected the latent violence beneath the surface of Colombian society. That violence emerged once again in 1810 with the movement for independence. For the following sixteen years the entire region was dominated by confusion and conflict. When Creole leaders of Bogotá attempted to dominate the entire viceroyalty, they met with intense resentment from other regions. Cartagena chose to remain under Spanish control rather than to submit to the dominance of the highland city. By 1817 the struggle had degenerated into cruel and senseless guerrilla warfare with atrocities committed by all factions. Economic and political disruptions paved the way for the campaigns of Simón Bolívar from Venezuela in 1819, resulting in the achievement of independence. The struggle to end colonial rule left a colorful military tradition in both conventional and guerrilla warfare, and a lasting fear of military institutions. With the success of the movement for independence, there was not a corresponding end to factionalism and conflict. Bolívar failed to hold the state together, and following his fall, a series of ambitious *caudillos* vied for power. Two major political factions, both dominated by the Creole elite, developed into the Liberal and Conservative parties.

The Conservatives defended religion as the cornerstone of society and insisted that the state must be based upon a strong central authority. The Liberals denounced clerical interference in secular affairs and insisted upon a weak government made up of virtually autonomous states. Often, the ideals of both factions were only a smokescreen for ambitious local bosses. Conflicts between the parties continually disrupted the political institutions and the nation's economy.

After the Constitution of 1886 theoretically ended the issue of federalism by providing for a highly centralized government, the two parties remained as rival feudal networks, the faction in power always imposing its will in city and village through violence and control of patronage. Dominance of the political machinery by the party in control made it impossible for the opposition to gain power except by force. The feuding between Liberals and Conservatives reached a climax in the terrible War of a Thousand Days (1899-1902), which took perhaps fifty thousand lives.

After the fighting ended, the Conservative Party remained firmly entrenched for the next twenty-eight years. Under its leadership, the nation experienced a period of unprecedented stability and economic growth stimulated to a large degree by extensive foreign investments.

In 1907 a vitally important set of military reforms professionalized the Colombian army. Officers were trained in the Military Cadet School in Bogotá, with further experience for senior officers at the nearby Superior War College. Laws were passed to remove the military man from politics, to standardize pay and conscription, and to place promotion and retirement upon a regulated basis. Although organization and tactics were adopted from the German Army model, many customs and procedures were retained from the roots of Colombia's own authentic military history. Military units were authorized to perform civic-action missions such as road building, establishment of prison colonies, and construction of public facilities. Procedures were formulated to permit the army to intervene in time of civil disorder, under presidential authority, on a politically neutral basis.

Significantly, the police remained small, decentralized, ineffective for internal-order missions, and highly political in nature. In 1928 there was a strike by the banana workers of the Atlantic coastal area where pay and living conditions were wretched. The local police were incompetent and unable to control the violence. The army was sent in under presidential declaration of military law and quickly revealed its inability to handle the unruly crowds. With minimal manipulation by Communist Party terrorists, the situation went out of control and army troops shot down dozens of rioting workers and even innocent bystanders. These events helped to prepare the stage for a renewal of more widespread violence in the decades to come.

In 1930 the ruling Conservative Party was split between two rival presidential candidates, thus making it possible for the Liberals to seize control of the executive branch of the government with only a minority vote. Long out of office, the Liberals were often vindictive and their policemen were highly politicized. Throughout the nation, Liberal officials were appointed at every level of the bureaucracy. Partisan feuding erupted in many regions. In some twenty months of fighting approximately ten thousand persons were killed, and only a patriotic outburst surrounding the Leticia imbroglio on the border with Peru in 1932 saved Colombia from the eruption of *la violencia* at that time.

World War II brought economic recovery to most sectors of the nation, and the Liberal Party continued to maintain political control.

In 1946 the reverse fluke put the minority Conservatives in power, but this time they had the tactics of their own Falangist elements to offset the two-fisted methods of the Liberals, who received fitful support from the Communists. In a thousand towns, isolated incidents grew into killing; this became Phase I of *la violencia*. For two years, the fighting continued in Santander, Norte de Santander, Boyacá, and Cundinamarca. Then, in April, 1948, with dangerous social tensions visible to foreign observers in Bogotá for the IXth Inter-American Conference, an insane man killed Jorge Eliécer Gaitán, hero of the Liberal masses. Liberals, Conservatives, and Communists poured their goon squads into the streets for an orgy of killing, looting, and mob fighting. The army stopped the rioting and saved the government, but there were three dangerous results of this social explosion, which became known as the *bogotazo*. Prisons were opened by mobs, freeing hundreds of criminals and political grudge fighters. Policemen of Liberal background revolted; and hundreds of police deserters and rebels discharged from the force took their weapons to the hills and became guerrillas. Tension between Liberals and Conservatives became so strong that local Liberal politicos began to form or support guerrilla forces, while local Conservatives began to organize vigilante gangs to attack Liberals.

Phase II of *la violencia* began near the end of 1948, when Liberals of the rural middle class formed guerrilla units in Boyacá. Taking advantage of the guerrilla tradition in the *llanos orientales*, they found the big cattle ranchers willing to support rebel units. Gradua y the guerrillas moved into eastern Boyacá and Meta. At peak strength in 1952, there were about twenty thousand of them in the eastern plains. During the same period, Liberals organized about six thousand guerrillas in Antioquia; and the Communists armed about five hundred men in the Cunday-Sumpapaz regions along the Tolima-Cundinamarca border, using as a base a group of peasant farmers' leagues that party elements had established in the 1930s.

The combined effort of these three guerrilla regions, and several more of purely bandit character, may be called the First Guerrilla War. The army remained small and mostly neutral, while the decentralized police forces grew in size and were heavily implicated in political fighting.

The army was an uneasy bystander as the people chose

sides between the two-fisted Conservative administration or their equally uncompromising Liberal opponents. The Conservatives rigged the 1950 election and tried to quell armed revolt with police repression. Viciously counterproductive methods were used, such as reprisal killings against uninvolved Liberals and the masquerading of police in army uniforms to fool the peasants.

By the early 1950s the army had separated Liberal guerrillas from savage police elements in the central and western mountain chain, but Liberal guerrillas in the sparsely populated eastern plains took over virtual control of several regions. Whether or not the police were professional in their operations, they were functionally unable to reassert control. As a result, even though army leaders disapproved of the partisan way in which the administration tried to employ military units, it became necessary for army units to engage both Liberal guerrillas and bandit groups in combat.

Gradually, the army was pressured into abandoning low-violence methods. After more than two highly frustrating years with little success against the insurgents, the army adopted a scorched-earth policy, burning villages and taking action against the people somewhat indiscriminately. The results were self-defeating, and the consciences of many officers were bothered. Responsible civilian leaders and army leaders began searching for new ways to make peace among the warring civilian factions.

In June, 1953, General Gustavo Rojas Pinilla overthrew the Laureano Gómez administration amid a general national euphoria. He negotiated a surrender of guerrillas in exchange for amnesty (*la entrega*), and he established some highly effective social services for the rural zones. He cracked the police forces into line by nationalizing them under the Ministry of War. But there his achievements ended.

It was during this second phase of *la violencia* that Sergeant Buitrago witnessed, in his boyhood, the widespread repression of many citizens in the predominantly Liberal Department of Valle. Conservatives were few in number in that region and often felt the sting of vengeance from Liberals, who were smarting under the lash of governmental repressions.

Rojas Pinilla thought that military neutralism could also function as an apolitical military government. Conservative elements saw their chance to perpetuate themselves in power and encouraged him to promote to high posts military officers who were sympathetic to Conservative beliefs. Starting in 1954, the army was hurled against the peasant leagues in Tolima, and this action grew into Phase III of *la violencia*. Slowly the fighting spread westward, so that by 1956 the Communist Party's military power was broken, but a whole generation of savage young *violentos* were leading rural Mafia-type gangs in the central and western *cordilleras*. Total killing was lower in this phase, and more confined geographically, but the fighting was also more savage. The armed forces united with the political parties to oust Rojas in time to redeem their credit; a military *junta* sent out another amnesty call, ending Phase III of *la violencia* (sometimes called the Second Guerrilla War).

It was during these years that the young Buitrago, a student at *colegio* (schooling roughly equivalent to both high school and junior college in the U.S. system) suffered the murder of his father. Whether the killing was political or purely criminal in nature, Buitrago saw it as the work of his country's enemies. He dedicated himself to a particular kind of priesthood—the defense of governmental institutions—and, after brief service as a civilian assistant to army units in Valle, he enlisted.

In 1958 the *junta* kept its word, turning over governance to the new National Front Coalition, under which the two parties would alternate four presidential terms and share all patronage equally. President Alberto Lleras Camargo declared that reduction of *la violencia*, which was now manifesting itself as deeply institutionalized banditry, was the top priority of business. His many political successes were not matched by reduction of *la violencia*, for many regional politicians were disgracefully compromised in murder and payoff with the *bandoleros*.

The army added a new dimension, that of the politically neutral, humanist force engaged in rural peacekeeping and nation building—to its tradition of apoliticism. As Guillermo León Valencia assumed the presidency in 1962, the army unfolded its program to curb Phase IV of *la violencia*.

The application of the Colombian Army to violence reduction through a novel framework was a modern expansion of the old schoolboy's adage:

Colombia es una nacion de cosas muy singulares;
Los civiles dan la guerra, y la paz los militares.

Colombia is a nation of very unusual things
Where civilians make war and soldiers make peace.

Working under civilian supervision, and in conjunction with several civilian agencies, the army launched a drive to restore civilization to the rural zones. Social and economic assistance was given by military units. Soldiers taught school, manned medical facilities, transported peasants to market, and negotiated wage increases with irresponsible landowners. Gang infiltrators joined the *bandoleros*, bringing them out of the hills to capture or ambush. About a dozen bandit chieftains had compromised the legal system sufficiently to become untouchable folk heroes who murdered at will; these were shot down in low-intensity combat operations.

Each bandit chief marked for violent treatment had already evaded the legal system by threatening the lives of rural judges, witnesses, and jailers through gang tactics. Several were under legal protection of elected members of the Congress or the departmental legislatures, camping on the land of these elected officials (thereby gaining legal immunity) and terrorizing their patrons' political rivals.

The success of the army in redeeming civilization for the peasants raised the question: why would not civilians undertake these tasks? As Phase IV of *la violencia*, the era of institutionalized banditry, drew to a close in June, 1965, the answer was still not visible.

Sergeant Buitrago worked his way gradually from the routine existence of an enlisted artilleryman into the sophisticated role of an intelligence operative, specializing in penetrating bandit gangs by posing as one of their own kind. Much of the detail in Buitrago's account is obviously omitted in deference to military secrecy. Combat veterans who read the account may well suspect that Buitrago brags or exaggerates from time to time.

Buitrago's life, from 1960 to mid-1965, was a continuing series of dangers, tribulations, and remarkable adventures. Undoubtedly Buitrago's imagination occasionally worked overtime in recounting his adventures, although there is documentary substantiation for many of his incredible exploits in breaking up several murderous bandit gangs.

Indeed, there was documentation enough to substantiate the award of the rare and coveted Cross of Boyacá, seldom granted for the type of unconventional fighting that has characterized *la violencia*. Buitrago received the medal from the hands of President León Valencia in a day of national recognition, during the climax of a costly, controversial, and often unpopular antibandit campaign that closed out *la violencia* as an identifiable phenomenon.

While Colombia was established politically as a constitutional democracy ruled by civilians, the dynamics of this arrangement could not stand unaltered under the onslaught of *la violencia*. If generals were ordered by their civilian commander-in-chief to make war on civilian groups for political reasons, they were forced to disobey civilian orders or use their military power in a partisan form. If the captain in a village stood idly by while civilian groups and police committed murder, he either intervened or allowed the killing to go on, thereby violating constitutional mandates in either case.

The point is that while the army used excessive force during three periods of *la violencia* (in the eastern plains in 1950–51, and in Tolima in 1955–56 and again in 1964), most of the time its small units were seen by rural Colombians as the peacemakers. And peacemakers cannot always be constitutional purists.

Sergeant Buitrago is a new type of soldier, different in many ways from the John Wayne image of World War II era cinematic origins, and also different from the swaggering, much-caricatured image of the *latino* military professional. Forged in the fires of *la violencia*, he became a guardian of constitutionalism among political extremists and criminals. Several Colombian officers have articulated their country's anti-*violencia* doctrines more explicitly, but Buitrago gives us a segment of his own life. He is more than the Wyatt Earp legend, even at its romanticized best; different as a soldier from Alvin York or Audie Murphy; and more complex than the James Bond character. Buitrago was also a braggart, an adventurer, a romantic, an unbending patriot, and a man who took self-righteous pleasure in killing the identified enemies of public order.

In all, there were only a few dozen men in the bandit gang-penetration program, and most of them worked in the VIIIth Brigade Zone (mainly the Department of Caldas, later divided into Caldas, Quindio, and Risaralda) from 1963 to 1966. They killed several dozen *bandoleros*, all known murderers, many of whom surely would have escaped conviction to kill again because of the sadly compromised legal system. They saved thousands of lives and recovered millions of pesos; several of these special operatives were killed, and most were wounded more than once.

Sergeant Buitrago is now medically retired. His story merits serious attention from those who are concerned about the maintenance of liberty and safety in the turbulent backlands of many nations.

RUSSELL W. RAMSEY

Prologue

A BOOK FOR EVERYONE

Sergeant 2nd Class Evelio Buitrago Salazar, member of the Artillery, which was known in the time of Louis XIV as the *ultima ratio regum,* submits to the readers the compilation of his memoirs, a succession of events he experienced during the difficult years of struggle against *bandolerismo.*

He is a soldier through and through. The account of his activities in the Quindío, in Valle del Cauca, and in Tolima is stripped of vanity and devoid of exaggeration and this speaks well of the author, who wears, for his merits, the Cross of Boyacá. With no intent to diminish the well-deserved fame of Sergeant Buitrago, who personifies the courageous spirit of the Colombian noncom, I can state that in the fascinating episodes or chapters of his book our men in arms can find part of their own lives, some of their own deeds, performed in different times and places in behalf of social peace and order.

It has been said that in Colombia the civilians make war and the soldiers make peace. This singular paradox throws a certain light on our civilian attitude and transforms the army into the "armed hand of the Constitution."

In their efforts to restore peace to the cities and countryside the military and police forces for several years have been giving their best: youth, enthusiasm and even their own blood. What more could be asked of those who with such careful impartiality serve at the altars of the country?

The peace of God, preached with unequaled love in the Sermon on the Mount, has returned to the Republic of Colombia, and the spawn of barbarism, cornered, pursued to its lair, and destroyed, is barely the sad memory of an epoch that must never be repeated.

As the author states very clearly in this book, which in my opinion would be a valuable addition to any library, military or civilian, he does not study the causes of *la violencia*, and this is as it should be, in order to avoid polemics that, after all, would not reveal the truth but rather would arouse passions and transform the smoldering ashes into devastating flames.

In this work we see the soldier using his arms in defense of guaranteed social rights, just as the Liberator decreed it from San Pedro Alejandrino. Reread each scene, each page, and you will find only the professional and the plain soldier, both seeking justice, carrying out their duty—the greatest aspiration of those who with honor don the uniform.

Herein also is described the *bandolero* of this hemisphere, divested of the attributes of valor and romanticism, which he never possessed. And let it be clear I am not talking about the true *guerrillero*; that is, the *paisano* who makes war, motivated by an ideal and who fights fiercely and independent of the regular armies. *"Zarpazo": Otra Cara de la Violencia* reveals the festering wound that threatened our society with death and indicates the medicine, strong, and painful, but necessary if the patient is to be saved.

For the first time in print the *bandoleros* appear without the attractions attributed to them by shallow writers, those absurd visionaries and deceived dreamers. Here the *bandoleros* file by in their frightening reality, lacking in wholesome aspirations, with no proper cause for rebellion. Crudeness, cruelty, greed, avarice, and great doses of perversity, treachery, cowardice, ignorance and rapine, ferocity and madness—these are the trappings of the *bandolero*.

In Colombia, a country well endowed geographically and demographically, in an unfortunate moment in her history, there appeared the *bandolero*—this sinister personage who found an easy way to live by attacking in gangs, robbing, killing, and kidnapping—encysted in regions vital to the national economy. The *bandolero*, a true excrescence upon democracy, but never its resultant, is the consequence of prolonged and bloody political controversies.

Had it not been for the energetic intervention of the armed forces Colombia would have bled itself to death; I do not exaggerate when I say that Colombia would have disappeared, because emissaries of foreign doctrines, taking advantage of *la violencia* as a bridge stretching between Asia and America, would have arrived at the land of Santander and Nariño; and then, instead of the tricolor that Miranda left us, the flags flying would bear the hammer and sickle.

Over the innumerable graves senselessly filled by *la violencia*, there rise hundreds of crosses that witness to the holocaust of officers, noncommissioned officers, soldiers, agents, and investigators. Eternal gratitude is owed them, martyrs to the cause of peace and concord.

May our children and our children's children never see the barbarism we have witnessed. May this book, with its many lessons, contribute to the preservation of the peace of God; may it help to echo through the years and over the length and breadth of our land the message of the Christmas angel: Peace among men.

My sincere congratulations to Sergeant Buitrago on these pages, which in a felicitous manner retrace his steps, steps as firm and brave as those of the courageous soldiers of the "Rifles," the "Vencedor," the "Voltígeros"—consecrated battalions that illuminated the route of Bolívar in our great struggle for independence, and which now add new laurels to their glorious standards in the Quindío and in Valle del Cauca.

GUILLERMO PLAZAS OLARTE,
COLONEL (RET.)

I dedicate this book
to the Armed Forces of
Colombia, to my wife,
and to my daughters.
The author

Zarpazo

1 · I Was Born in Sevilla

*A land of singular beauty, rich and prosperous is
Valle del Cauca.*

I was born in Sevilla and spent my childhood there, in one of
the most fertile corners of the department of Valle del
Cauca. This city rightly has been called the coffee capital of
Colombia.*

My father, good *sevillano* that he was, owned a piece of
land, part pasture, part with banana trees on it, a short
distance out of town. We were not wealthy people or by any
means part of what might be called the ruling class, but we
owned our house and made up with work what we lacked in
luck. My mother, from an old Pereira family, self-sacrificingly
took excellent care of her numerous family, as the women
from Caldas do so well. In short, I come from an average and
typical family of the high Quindío region—enterprising, hard
working, believers in God.

Sevilla had a population of some seventy thousand in
1936, the year I was christened. The city, with its houses of
bamboo and wood and standing some forty-six hundred feet
above sea level, enjoyed a moderate climate well suited for
growing the plant that is the base of the Colombian
economy—the coffee tree.

Coffee everywhere—coffee beans drying in the midday sun;
coffee ground and packaged, impregnating stores and sheds

NOTE: Footnotes marked by an asterisk (*) are those of the author.
The interpretive footnotes indicated by a dagger (†) are the work of the
editor.

Note also that in these memoirs some names have been changed or disguised for reasons of security or convenience.

*Sevilla, an important city in the department of Valle del Cauca, is
called "the coffee capital of Colombia." According to the official
estimate, Sevilla had a population of 100,000 in June 1963. Geographically, it belongs to the well-endowed region of the Quindío, a zone vital
to the economy of the country, since coffee continues to be the base of
Colombia's wealth.

with its aroma. The smell of coffee wafted from the roads accompanying the jerky gait of the mules and the shouts of the drivers. The smell of coffee pervading homes and warehouses. The aroma rising from the heated brew to ascend to the heavens!

In the surrounding countryside grew the coffee trees, guarded by banana trees or shaded by the branches of the *guamos*. The mild coffee of Sevilla that filled the fiber sacks and the baskets with red cherries; that put calluses on the fingers of the workers; that rewarded well those who harvested it, depulped it, dried it and packaged it; that crossed the seas of the world to distant ports, where it was converted into dollars!†

So it was in Sevilla in the year of grace 1936, with the sky full of clouds, like flags of truce spread out over the spurs of the cordillera. A place for working, for making money, with long streets lined with shops and stores, inns, garages, blacksmith shops, banks, schools, hospitals, and churches. A place for living intensely, where one studied or carried on business, where one bartered or sold, where one ate good corn cakes and real stew. A land for rich and poor, a land of elegant women and independent men! A land of fine horses and even better mules, of horse traders and horse breakers, where one could take a brandy and play billiards at any hour. A place where one put a dime in the juke box and danced to the blaring music with the painted girls who made more than one fellow lose his head in the cantinas and the houses of entertainment!

Sevilla, a city blessed by nature, had taken shape as the woodcutters felled the trees, cleared the underbrush and burned the debris to make that fertile ground a part of Colombia.

---

†There are here two paradoxes that are difficult to explain. One is the fact that these same sturdy middle-class farmers provided more support for the *bandoleros* during Phase IV of *la violencia* than did the impoverished tenant farmers from several other regions. The other is that overdependency upon coffee, necessary as a cash crop for internal development, has retarded economic diversification.

2 · Artillery

Artilleryman, march on bravely.

I am a sergeant 2nd class in the artillery.

My emblem is black like the mouths of the howitzers. I say without hesitancy that during the greater part of my service my battalion was the Fourth, called the San Mateo. My specialty, for those interested in specifics, is intelligence and topography; however, I am well acquainted with the guns, the sighting techniques, the firing procedures, the horses—in sum, everything a sergeant 2nd class ought to know.

I am an artilleryman and the taste of gunpowder is in my blood, that is why I repeat the motto with emotion: DUTY BEFORE LIFE! When I put on the uniform with the gleaming crossed cannon on my jacket, I walk briskly, my head erect, convinced of the importance of my shoulder patch.

I am a noncommissioned officer in the Colombian army, and proud of it! This year, the year I am writing my memoirs, I hope to be promoted to sergeant 1st class.† Then I shall add a black diamond to my chevrons.

For ten years I have been in service—two five-year hitches, in which destiny placed me face to face with *la violencia*. I know it through experience; I have tracked it; I have followed its bloody trail and I have paused with anguish before its destructive work, its wreckage, ruin and ashes.

Furthermore, in carrying out the orders of my superiors, I have gone to the backlands and pretended to be a *bandolero*.

I know about *la violencia* and about its horrors, which remind me of the frightening saying of the ancients: "The bite of the sepent does not harm the serpent; only man is wolf to man."

---

†Buitrago was eventually promoted to the highest enlisted rank and retired from active service.

I have done guard duty in army bases and also I have been a lookout for the outlaws' den. My hand—why not go ahead and say it?—has punished monsters whose countless victims could not be avenged by society; those monsters, those regrettably notorious delinquents whom some of the scientific specialists of the "new wave" have tried to defend.†

I know *la violencia*, which took my father's life, devoured my uncles, and diminished my inheritance.

I am, then, one of so many soldiers whose lot it was to deal with the criminals.

Here are my memoirs, pared down to the bare facts. I have written them so that my compatriots may know the other side of the coin, and may study it and render a verdict.

Miguel de Unamuno has already expressed my feeling: "With the timbers of remembrance we build our hopes."

If my memoirs serve a good purpose, let God and country reward me, and if they do not, let God and country call me to account!

3 · La Rochela

To earn one's bread by the sweat of one's brow . . .

Far from Colombia, I am writing these memoirs in Lima, the beautiful capital of Peru. I am two thousand kilometers from

---

†Buitrago refers here to the team of sociologists that gathered data on *la violencia* in 1958–1959 and published landmark studies in 1962 and 1964. They were: Dr. Orlando Fals Borda, Ph.D. (University of Florida), then chairman of the Sociology Faculty, National University; Dr. Eduardo Umaña Luna, legal sociologist of the Sociology Faculty, National University; and Monsignor Germán Gúzman Campos, priest in the *violencia*-ridden town of Libano, Tolima. The viewpoint was neo-Marxist, with the *bandoleros* presented as the victims of an immorally governed society.

my homeland; here nothing or no one can exert influence to alter the impartiality of my account. A muffled noise rises unceasingly from Arequipa Avenue, traversed in both directions by endless strings of automobiles. The splendor of summer has already passed; the sky is gray and a humidity of 95 percent envelops the land of Pizarro. My thoughts suddenly turn to my father's farm, the *finca* La Rochela.

By dint of his own industry my father became owner of a hacienda near Belén de Umbria, which supplied us with enough to live. However, the large family meant more and more expenses. My parents must have talked about it long and hard before they decided to swap the *finca* in the western part of Caldas† for another property, La Rochela, located in Aures, a municipality of Caicedonia.

In 1953, the change was decided upon, and my mother moved to Cali with five daughters and three young sons. One of my brothers was doing his military service in the *llanos*, and the oldest, out on his own, managed a pharmacy.

To support us in Cali, the new *finca* had to produce, and our expenses really increased as it became necessary to multiply by eight the cost of tuition, books, supplies, and uniforms. That is why my father remained alone at La Rochela, the land on which all of his hopes rested. He was a real man! True, the terrain was very broken, but, gullies and all, we had thirty *plazas* of coffee trees, watered in part by the torrential Barragán and crossed by ravines and arroyos that twisted into S's before they disappeared around a bend. The coffee trees were bordered by sour and sweet guavas, avocados, orange and mandarin trees, sapodillas, soursops, *chirimoyos* and banana trees. Here and there, testifying to the productivity of the moderate climate, were the *churimo*, the *carbonero*, the balsam, the *surrumbo*, and clumps of the giant bamboo, which supplied rails for fences and framing for buildings.

A generator provided electricity for the big house—with porches and landscaping, where my father lived—and for four

---

†The department of Caldas, during the years of Buitrago's tale, embraced the present departments of Caldas, Quindío, and Risaralda.

other buildings. These, which were also ours, were used as barracks for a military post, as a school, and as bosses' quarters. Frequently we would leave Cali and visit the *finca*. By the time the sun was coming up over the mountains the cows were already milked, the horses were saddled, and the packsaddles were on the mules, ready to take the coffee to market, where it sold for twenty-five pesos per *arroba*.*

Sometimes we found horses lazily circling the cane press, turning it to make the cane juice drip into five boiling pots that were heated by fires of brush or dry cane stalks. At night, the wind carried the aroma of syrup and fresh sugar cakes. The plumed roosters, as if they had some part in the enterprise, proclaimed their jubilation over the success of the grinding.

That is the way the work went at La Rochela—with perseverance, with happiness, with enthusiasm. Not far away was the town to which the surly mules bore the brown sugar [*panela*] by the pound, and the coffee by the *arroba*, which gave my father the money he needed to send to Cali.

The latch string was always out to anyone who wanted to do a day's work at the hacienda; there was no odious political discrimination.

When the work was done a lad would strike some joyful chords on the tiple [soprano guitar] or venture a *bambuco*.

Sundays the workers went to church with the *patrón*, to give thanks and, after church, to buy the next week's necessities.

The peace of God prevailed there until, one day . . .

---

*The price of an *arroba* of coffee (roughly twenty-five pounds), in the latter half of 1965, according to the Coffee Growers Federation, was seventy-three and a half pesos.

4 · *La Violencia* is Manifest

*The shrimp that falls asleep will be carried along by
the current.*

During the latter part of 1953 and most of 1954 we Colombians enjoyed complete peace. The bonfires ignited by hatred had been put out. Of course, as a consequence of an "undeclared civil war," there remained gangs of hoodlums, more or less neutralized by the government's amnesty, but potentially active, especially in the central mountains.†

These hoodlums, sustained by the abundant supplies and wherewithal easily acquired in assaults and holdups, were awaiting only the right moment to resume their activities. That moment came, nobody knows just how.

Chispas, Sangre Negra, Conrado Salazar, Gata, Melco, Polancho, and other antisocial types from the lower ranks of the brigand mafia were responsible for the mourning black worn by many citizens all through the departments of Caldas, Tolima, and Valle.

Some countrymen—and sad it is to say so—followed the basilisk to line their own pockets and attain some desired position or status.

Let the sociologists make their detailed studies and exhaustive analyses of the causes of the new violence. Confound then, with their interesting theories! What is sure is that the *bandoleros* appeared—men dedicated to pillage, robbery, murder, kidnapping, extortion; individuals without ideals, without feelings, placed by their own choice beyond the pale of the law, both human and divine.

---

†Buitrago refers here to *la entrega*, a political arrangement under which the Rojas Pinilla administration allowed anyone under arms to turn himself in to the army, exchanging his weapon for a blanket legal amnesty. The "central mountains" to which he refers are, essentially, the Department of Tolima, where military heavy-handedness, Communist party subversive efforts, and endemic poverty soon led to new warfare.

Familiar with the terrain, they laughed at the operations of the military, and they made use of the ambush with great effectiveness. Aided by the fear of those whose lives and haciendas they threatened, they took possession of the fertile land, they exacted tribute, they carried off women, and they killed anyone who tried to stop them.

Just to introduce these merciless monsters would be more than enough for this book, but there are more important considerations. Outside this country good people, and even esteemed authors, are ill-informed about the lives and incredible deeds of the *bandoleros,,* and this lack of knowledge obliges me to describe them as they should be described.

I was in the fourth year of my *bachillerato*† at the Colegio de Santa Librada in Cali. Things were going very well for my mother and my brothers and sisters in Sultana, but in Aures they were going from bad to worse. There were rumors, *boletos* (extortion notes or threatening notes), threats; people were abandoning their rural *fincas* in droves! A typical *boleto* was this one, which my father received:

> Don Luis, watch your step. It will be better for your health to sell or rent out your *finca*. There are none of your party left in this part of the country!

The devil take them and their threats, thought my father. Could he really be harming society, living as God commands and the constitution of Colombia provides? Were not those extortionists just lurking around, ready to buy from him for practically nothing the hacienda into which he had put everything?

Because my father was courageous, because he kept things orderly at his settlement, because he let the military use one of his buildings as a barracks, because he allowed the little country school to be held on his property, and because

---

†In Colombia, the *"bachillerato"* is the general equivalent of the United States junior-college certificate or degree.

he did not give in to the hoodlums, the latter resolved to eliminate him.

The first Sunday of August 1955 he went to the monthly *feria* [fair] at Génova to buy some milch cows. Sanguine, as always, he trotted along on his fine horse, never imagining that on his way back from the *feria* five assassins would empty their revolvers into his body.

Two workers who were accompanying him picked him up and carried him back to La Rochela as quickly as possible. There, fighting death, he managed to dictate a letter to his children, identifying his attackers.

When the fateful news reached the halls of Santa Librada, I was overcome with grief and rage. I wept for a long time and then, without telling anyone, I went to the *finca* as fast as I could. Too late! When I arrived my father had already died. Judging that nothing would be served by my remaining with the dear, dead body, I did not stay for the burial. I knew who the murderers were. So buckling on a revolver and clutching the damning letter in my hand, I headed for the backlands to find them.

And where does the law allow . . .? my conscience was asking me. True, the legal authorities had the responsibility for catching the five assassins. But who could guarantee, things being the way they were in Aures, that the inspector and his deputies would be successful in their investigations? Wasn't it true that many crimes went unpunished? *I* would find the killers. *I* would match forces with them and take my vengeance!

For two weeks, day and night, I stayed in the bush, constantly watching, going from *finca* to *finca*, skulking around the coffee plantations. I located three of those on the list, but, knowing that the judges would not condone reprisals, I went to the military post for help. Reason had triumphed over my rashness.

I went with a patrol from the Palacé Battalion, serving them as guide. At the hacienda La Suiza we captured two. They confessed: "Yes! We killed him on orders from don N.N. from Cumbarco."

As the returning patrol passed near El Paraíso, we were ambushed. Several soldiers fell. We took cover. One of the attackers, whom I later identified as another of the five who murdered my father, was riddled in a burst of our fire. Just as the rain of lead reached its peak, our two prisoners tried to get away. It always happens this way.

I do not know whether it was the revolvers or the Mauser rifles that scored bull's-eyes on the moving targets. On the crumpled, dirty letter my pencil crossed out three names!

At the end of two months I located the other killers near the Buena Vista Settlement. When they saw us—I was with a friend—they opened fire. There was no time to notify the authorities. The exchange of fire lasted half an hour. We turned over to the local police a 7 mm. Mauser rifle and a Gras from the War of a Thousand Days.†

In those days I was not a soldier, but I cooperated with the government; perhaps in my own way I was practicing *auto-defensa*.* For one of the slain *bandoleros* the government of the Department of Caldas had offered a sizeable reward. We were living the second *violencia*.**†

---

†The Gras was a 9 mm. single-shot French Army rifle, firing a heavy, pure-lead slug, with great accuracy and tremendous knock-down power. It was built for the Franco-Prussian War of 1870, and several thousand were purchased for the Colombian Army before the close of the nineteenth century. During the Colombian War of a Thousand Days (1899–1902) the Gras played a big role. Old models continued in use well into *la violencia*.

Auto-defensa: The defense of the villages through their own militia organizations facilitates and lightens the task of the national security forces, making possible the use of the latter in critical places. The creation of an understanding of *auto-defensa* is a laborious and long-range task; the concept requires support of the people; it must be democratic in character and have sufficient strength and the support of legal forces. *Auto-defensa* has been established in several places in Colombia with excellent results.

**In some regions of the country they speak of the "First" *Violencia* and the "Second," and even of the "Third"; the First took place be-

5 · The Catch

*The barracks is the university of the common
people.*

I did not go back to school. Instead, I took charge of the
work at the *finca*. But on those occasions when I had to be
absent the *bandoleros* would raid La Rochela, and with a
vengeance! Once they killed seven workers and two women.
Wise men have observed that "violence begets violence."
How true! N.N., the man who had originated the plot to kill
my father, had flown from Cumbarco. A cousin of mine followed him, however, and passing himself off as a worker
from a hacienda between Sevilla and Caicedonia, found the
opportunity to kill him and thus avenge my father's murder.
The police subsequently killed my cousin.

Against my wishes I had to leave La Rochela and return
to Cali. On February 20, 1956, as the audience was leaving
the Alcázar Theater, some sixty of us were herded together in
a conscription round-up and taken under heavy guard to the
barracks in the Pichincha Battalion, at that time located in
the heart of the city.

It was interesting to watch the different emotional reactions of the forced conscripts. Some told jokes; others were
obviously worried; some kept repeating that their parents

tween 1948 and 1953, and the Second was unleashed in 1954.

†During Phase II and Phase III of *la violencia* there was a strong clash
between Conservative administrations in Cali and the Liberal majority
in the Department of Valle. Starting with the assumption of command
over the Army's 3rd Brigade by (then) Colonel Gustavo Rojas Pinilla,
the Army tended to favor Conservatives in that region. Buitrago's
family, as members of the Conservative minority in their area,
undoubtedly held a privileged relationship. There is little doubt, however, that Buitrago's father was murdered, without any motive other
than vengeance, by Liberals who were smarting under the Conservative
administration.

were dead and that they were the sole support of their families. These were smoking; those over there were just staring. Practically everybody was talking about the happenings of the day—about the kidnappings, about the perilous life of the militia, about the *bandolero* arms caches that had been found.

The medical examination the next day found me suitable. I was resolved to do my military service in any event, whether as a volunteer or however it might be.

The draft dodgers and those who put on the uniform much against their will call those who volunteer *"regalados,"* a word suggesting that one "presents" himself and also that one is a sissy. That epithet had so much venom in it that many such youths avoided visiting the barracks so as not to be taunted by their acquaintances in such a pejorative way.

It is a curious thing that in certain towns clever young men, clever but without an ounce of patriotism, avoid military service and are protected by the mayor, the solicitor, the treasurer, or the principal doctor, while the service schools fill their quotas with volunteers, who almost always make excellent soldiers. What guard-duty, army food, and binges they consign the Smith boy and Jones boy to so that the small-town slacker can be found medically "unfit" or receive "exemptions" not provided for in the law.†

Speaking for myself, I know that if they had not picked me up in the "catch" I would have volunteered that very year. In my heart, I *wanted* to put on the uniform of our army and to bear arms for the republic! I knew that our liberators of a hundred and fifty years before had volunteered for the battalions of liberty.

In 1956, of course, the war was not against troops from Spain who were, after all, defenders of a land that had been conquered and colonized by Castilians. Now the stability of our country's institutions was being threatened by another

---

†Buitrago reflects here the civil-military relationships around Valle. Other parts of Colombia—specifically, areas of Tolima, Boyacá, Santander, and the *llanos orientales*—produce every year hundreds of youngsters who consider military service a privilege.

enemy, an enemy fierce in his deviousness and encouraged, at times, by some of my own beclouded countrymen. It was a perilous, cruel struggle against bloodthirsty and ignorant adversaries, who have been called "heroes" by the authors of fawning, absurd "novels."†

As one who had seen the unburied corpses of country people and been infuriated by the injustice, I now wanted to be a soldier in order to pursue the *bandoleros* and to catch them or kill them. What did my life matter if I risked it valiantly to avenge so many lives already sacrificed?

I was thinking these things as my squad leader was making me march along the drill field. He monotonously kept repeating his cadence and commands: Left, two, three, four . . . ! They had sent us to Medellín.

6 · A Soldier in Company "D"

A soldier is a citizen that the law designates to be the guardian of public order and the nation's honor and other major interests. —General Mestre

The training schedule called for several weeks of basic individual training for the recruit and several weeks of advanced training. But around Puerto Berrío public order was in bad shape—*maluco* (*malucho*, "Sickly, sicklish") as they say in Antioquia. Consequently, after two months of training Company D was detached to pursue the *bandolero* Caballito. The truth is, we were not ready for the undertaking.

But, after all, how good it was to get away from the forced confinement of recruit life, even though it might mean a fight with the *bandoleros*.

---

†In 1956, and for a decade before that date, there was indeed genuine resistance to real repression. The "novels" that Buitrago here dismisses so breezily are often polemical but are also indicative of a struggle by men whose motives were not mere banditry.

The Magdalena River sweeps majestically past Puerto Berrío.† There one feels the tropics in all its intensity— burning sun, exhausting heat, storms that terrify with their deafening thunder and their lightning. In good weather the people come from the haciendas loaded down with products of the warm climate. the port is filled with traders, with white *ruanas*, with big hats, with wallets full of money.

From there the railroad goes to Medellín, a line over three hundred miles long and known throughout the country for its long tunnel, La Quiebra.

Puerto Berrío perpetuates the name of an illustrious son of the mountains, the glory and pride of Antioquia. In the tropical port the steamships *Naviera* and *Marvásquez* used to berth, resting on their long trips up and down the river. Those wonderful river voyages have been dealt a severe blow by the use of the airplane, and *la violencia* has given them the coup de grâce.

We men of Company D soldiered well, the captain told us. In some exciting patrolling we covered big haciendas, marshes, channels, rivers, and jungles. Caballito lost at least fourteen of his gang, that is, about a third. What a great pity that the region, so rich, where prize cattle grazed and where two crops a year could be harvested, should be in- fested with *bandoleros*.

We tracked them down, we hurt them, and we drove them from the vicinity. Then, carrying out a special assign- ment from our officers, four other soldiers and I took to the woods in civilian clothes. Mission accomplished! Three *bandoleros* killed and three service rifles recovered. For recruits, we certainly had not done badly!

---

†This river port, in the extreme western tip of the Boyacá "panhandle," was a center of furious resistance by Liberal and some Communist guerrillas during the 1948–1953 era. Much of the resistance had degen- erated into crime by the time of Buitrago's experiences there.

No, we were no longer mere recruits; we had gotten accustomed to the smell of gunpowder in several engagements.

They gave the five of us ten days' furlough.

Back at Medellín when I reported to S-1, a sergeant, a good fellow, said to me: "Don't you want to go to Pereira and be an artilleryman? We're going to be sending out a quota."

I was glad I had a tongue with which to say yes. "I sure do!" I replied, and so it was that in June 1956 the lieutenant sent me to Pereira.

7 · I Don't Play that Way, Colonel

Existence is the first good; and the second is the manner of existing.   —Simón Bolívar

Pereira, a city without doors, where there are no strangers and everybody is a *pereirano*. Thriving, enterprising Pereira vies with Manizales in population, progress, public spirit, and local pride.

One day the *pereiranos* said: Let's make our own airport! They did not turn to the government; instead they went—men, women, the old, the young—to Matecaña and raised enough money through benefits and donations to build the runway that at that time fulfilled their aspirations. But Pereira gets bigger with every dawning day, and now it is making plans for an international airport. Nobody doubts that *pereiranos*, if they continue thus, will surely be the first Colombians to reach the moon, where they will establish a branch of the Club Rialto.

Their patriotism aroused during the Independence, they resolved to pay tribute to the Liberator, and in singular homage they put in the plaza his statue, completely undraped—"the naked Bolívar," the masterpiece of our countryman Arenas Betancourt.

The ninth of April, when Colombia was shaken by the sacrifice of Jorge Eliécer Gaitán, Pereira was saved by the Army. The grateful citizens presented to the ministry of war the coffee plantation Maraya, where the artillery now has modern barracks.†

That is Pereira. If in material things it outstrips the estimates, in the spiritual it already has a bishop and there they say that it aspires to an archbishopric and a cardinal's hat.

I thought things would be fine in the San Mateo Battalion, but I was mistaken. I was hoping to continue to contribute my efforts to the restoring of peace to my countrymen. What a disappointment! They put me in the battery assigned to work on the *finca* Unidad. No! I was not of a mind to wield a hoe or prune bushes or pick coffee beans! If I had wanted to do that kind of manual labor I would have stayed in Sevilla, Valle, or in Cali.

The military is the military, of course, and orders must be carried out or else the military cannot exist. Even so, I felt some barracks fever, like that of my first months of service, and I could not understand why they made me work in agriculture.

One morning the colonel made the battery choose between working the coffee plantation and going hungry. Since the one who is in charge gives the orders, and since even suffering is tolerable if one has something to eat, we worked.

---

†On April 9, 1948, an insane indigent assassinated Liberal Party leader Jorge Eliécer Gaitán. Liberals, Conservatives, and Communists poured into the streets of Bogotá and several other cities, releasing prisoners, burning, looting, and killing several thousand people. Quick and heroic action by army units in several cities (such as Pereira) saved countless thousands of additional lives. National Police units were ineffective and, in some cases, joined the rioters. This event expanded *la violencia* in Colombia from a spotty rural phenomenon into a general condition in many parts of the country.

But generals give orders to colonels and soon we had a new colonel.

"Hey, buddy, the word is they're going to be sending people to a noncom school at Bogotá. I sure hope that's so!"

"If I get on the ball, would you recommend me, sergeant?"

Some days later, at the artillery school at La Picota, south of Bogotá, we were about to freeze to death, especially early in the morning. About the training and night exercises it is better to say nothing. From the bleak Cruz Verde plateau came torturing blasts of wind blowing a fine drizzle that went through our uniforms and pricked like needles. Then I would remember the pleasant climate of Pereira and think nostalgically of my old battalion.

But in Bogotá there were really good soldiers and from July to December, in company with sixty other trainees, I soaked up artillery lore, especially that having to do with the 75 mm. Skoda howitzer.

We graduated. I was second in the class and they gave me my first promotion.

Corporal 2nd Class! The dream of my first stripe, of my first command. Corporal 2nd, the first step up in a sacrificial profession, but a profession full of great satisfactions. Corporal 2nd, with the privileges of the noncom's club, frequent passes to town, and four hundred pesos for my wallet.

"Yes, Corporal!" "As you command, Corporal!" How much philosophy is contained in those words, which my soldiers henceforth would address to me—words that would remind me not only of my rank but also of my responsibility to the army. I would command a squad or a gun crew, and I would have under my direct command a group of men, in peace or war, in the colorful parades on national holidays or in surprise attacks against the *bandoleros*, in the close-order drill on the parade grounds or under the fire of enemy rifles.

They would name me Honor Noncom or outstanding corporal and before the admiring gaze of my companions I would render honors to the reviewing officers: "Detail, ATTENTION! Eyes RIGHT!"

Before the end of the year there was a call for volunteers
to go to Tolima. My heart beat faster, and at the thought of
that good land being tortured by *bandoleros*, I felt a desire to
fight them. Without thinking twice about it I said: "Tolima?
For there, yes. Here I am, Captain!"

8 · Ataco, as the Name Indicated

*It might be said that Tolima was formed by a blow
with the hand of a tremendous giant.*
                                        —Daniel Samper Ortega

It is written that the last emperor of the Western Empire, on
receiving word that barbarians had taken Rome, "was very
unperturbed and just turned over in bed when he became
aware that it was the capital of the Empire they meant and
not the rooster Rome, of which he was very fond" (*La
paciencia*, Marco Fidel Suárez).

Something like the emperor's attitude toward Rome is
felt, unfortunately, by many Colombians when they hear
reports of *la violencia*. If the attacks and the killings take
place in other departments or far from the local scene, they
just turn over in bed and, with unbelievable tranquility, go
right on sleeping. So ten people were killed in Roncesvalles?
And where is that? In Tolima? Those poor people!

As if the country were not one in its geography, in its
family of seventeen million members! As if those events,
which seem isolated, did not combine to produce this
trauma, so difficult to cure!

But what are we to do, if dust we are and to dust we
must return?

Let us recognize that the heightened intensity of *la
violencia* in certain regions of the country has been due to
the indifference of a good part of the population.

The common man expresses in a simple metaphor the

variety and beauty of our land, saying that in Colombia you couldn't steal anything that wouldn't be worthwhile. And what an axiomatic statement! Each department possesses delightful countryside and incalculable wealth: sea or river, snow-capped peaks or endless *llanos*, forests, or meadowlands, great *mesetas* or diamond-clear lakes.

Among the twenty-one departments of Colombia there is one whose nearly eighty-nine hundred square miles host nine hundred thousand inhabitants: Tolima.

When the plane traveler crosses the skies of Tolima in clear weather he admires the beauty of El Nevado, which towers over the range like a gigantic sentinel of the region. As one crosses the department by the road or horse trail he realizes that the hand of God has been lavish here in pouring out His gifts.

Because of its difficult terrain, Tolima was chosen by the *bandoleros* to be the theater of their lamentable and notorious operations. In reality, no other department has suffered so much as Tolima.† Its rivers mix their waters with the tears of the victims!

I was happy to be going to Tolima; I was sure there would be fighting. I was young, a bachelor, and I realized my country needed me. I just could not understand how some men could devote themselves to destruction when everything invited one to live by his own works in that fertile land; it was beyond me how some men band together for criminal purposes instead of uniting for progress.

Such thoughts were going through my mind as the trucks carried us over the rough road to the distant town of Ataco. Four noncoms—all volunteers—and sixty soldiers were assigned to the battery stationed there.

Ataco, the town; also *ataco*, the first personal singular, present indicative of the verb *atacar*, "to attack."

---

†While Buitrago is correct about the depth of suffering in *la violencia* in the department of Tolima, the *bandoleros* appeared in Tolima as a second-generation result of intense fighting there between the rural arm of the Colombian Communist Party and the Colombian Army.

On January 10, 1957, Lieutenant N. N. sent me and three other noncoms and twenty-eight soldiers on patrol. It was necessary to reconnoiter a canyon called "El Infierno," an imposing slit in the mountain range, bordered on each side by almost inaccessible peaks.

We were ambushed! I moved fast and with five soldiers managed to get out of the ambush and to counterattack. The patrol was saved, but at a cost of one noncom and four soldiers killed.

There was a military checkpoint at El Bosque, between Romerales and Juntas. The lieutenant selected me to be a sniper. Private Aponte and I spent three days and nights at a concealed observation post overlooking the route any *bandoleros* would have to use. We had good combat rations to eat.

We waited. Three of the enemy fell, and we recovered two rifles.

After the action came the comments, joyful or sad, depending on the outcome. "I came out of this alive," those of us who were safe and sound would say, just like the anxious passengers of an airplane when it finally lands safely.

We had orders to take our dead to the nearest military installation, but if there was danger we buried them temporarily on the spot—without flowers, without prayers, without holy water. And when we could, we also buried the bodies of our enemies.

We would have squad inspection, we would load our rifles, we would check our hand grenades, we would eat something, and then we would resume our patrolling.

Scouting the roads from Romerales, the lieutenant, three noncoms, and eighteen soldiers were ambushed. Things did not turn out as the enemy expected, however, because we killed seven of them, while we had to lament the death of only one comrade.

Why were the *bandoleros* unsuccessful? Because we now had more experience, because we were well commanded, and because my squad leader ordered us to throw our hand grenades at the right time.

We returned to the post carrying as trophies a Madsen submachine gun, three Grases, and some revolvers and pistols.

We lived, as pious ladies say, with the Credo on our lips and our lives hanging by a thread. Since I was not made of iron but of flesh and bone, and having spent many nights out in bad weather and been rain-soaked out in the field many times, I became ill. With my body racked by the effects of malaria and other illnesses, I went to the hospital of the Roock Battalion at Ibagué.

9 · Roock's Handsaw

Long live this country! Its dear earth will be my final resting place.   —Colonel James Roock

While convalescing from my illness, I wandered around the installations of the 18th Infantry Battalion, which is called the "Coronel Roock," a unit of our military forces that honors the memory of the English legionary, the martyr of the Pántano de Vargas.*

On one occasion, they were holding a deathwatch in the noncoms' club over the bodies of several soldiers killed by the *bandoleros*. As I stared at the flickering candles, I asked myself sorrowfully how may times that sad ceremony had been repeated there? Who would console the absent mothers, who perhaps at that very moment were counting the minutes

---

*The brave Colonel Roock, an Englishman by birth, took part in the Battle of Waterloo as an aide-de-damp to the Prince of Orange. He came to Venezuela in 1817 and served in Guyana with the rank of lieutenant colonel. In the campaign of 1818 he served on the General Staff. The following year, he was in the campaign in the *llanos* of Apure as a colonel commanding the corps of the British Legion. At the outset of the Nueva Granada campaign Roock told Bolívar, in a discussion of the desertion of some squadrons: "As commander of the British Legion, I shall follow your Excellency to Cape Horn, and beyond if necessary" (*Historia de Colombia*, Gerardo Arrubla and Jesús María Henao).

remaining until their sons would come back home?

A squad of seven riflemen and two noncoms would present arms in salute to the mortal remains and bugler would sound Taps. Then the grave would swallow up the bodies of those comrades. Afterward, a letter for the parents, a citation in the Orders of the Day, and a medal.

On one of the interior walls of the noncoms' club in Ibagué the painter Alberto Soto had painted his well-intentioned but historically inaccurate version of the sacrifice of the English officer, Roock. In the hand of Dr. Foley the artist had put a handsaw (*serrucho*) with which he had just amputated the arm of James Roock. From the stump fall drops of blood as the hero, with his other hand, holds aloft the severed arm in an unforgettable salute to the country that was to give him a final resting place. This scene was the back-drop at the wake for the dead soldiers.

Except for the mistake of the handsaw, instead of the bistoury, the surgeon's instrument, the painter would have been quite accurate. The records are clear when they speak of the doctors who came with the English legionaries hired through the initiative of our great Liberator, Simón Bolívar: Dr. Foley had brought along a full set of surgical instruments.

At any event, the painter had wanted to create an impression and he had succeeded in doing so to the point that, in the Sixth Brigade, in a twist of wry humor, they have given to the picture the title *"La violencia y el serrucho,"* as if to make a symbolic allusion to those who, in the name of *la violencia*, sever or destroy part of some productive facility, a criminal act that cries out to God for redress.

I requested a transfer to the San Mateo Battalion and it was granted.

10 · Holy Week and Patrolling

First duty, then devotions.

Maundy Thursday—hours of mourning, penitence, and prayer. The fervor of the Colombians in these holy days is so great that many compatriots in the *llanos* and the jungle who are not able to attend the religious services and the solemn processions (through circumstances beyond their control), honor the Lord by abstaining from all physical labor, from bathing their tired bodies in the streams, from slaughtering animals, and from singing their customary songs of love for their native soil.

At that time I belonged to the La Paloma military installation, a unit of the Cazadores Battalion. The stability of public order was threatened and so we had a strict rotation schedule of patrolling the steep slopes of Tolima.

On Maundy Thursday, after committing myself to God's care, I left the post with eighteen soldiers and four corporals 2nd class. As the saying goes, "Duty before devotions."

From early morning we followed the trail of some *bandoleros* who at that time were violating the holy days, as will be seen later on. In midafternoon, after some ten hours of fatiguing tracking, we stopped to eat. Since patrol duty sometimes lasted seventy-two hours at a stretch, after eating we selected a particular spot for our next objective.

"To Toche canyon . . . Move out!"

The scouts took a lead of about two hundred yards, but the pace had to be slow because we were traveling in enemy territory and, worse still, the fog that covered everything made our movements even more risky. I had just started to move off with the rest of my men when I heard a sound like the cry of a woman.

Our automatic rifleman, a black from Chocó, said to me: "Didn't you hear that, Corporal? Somebody crying?" A noncom said he had heard the same thing.

Thinking of all the things that might happen, I called the

scouts back and ordered a thorough reconnoitering of the terrain around us.

Another cry, like the first, came from somewhere. I crawled up to some *frailejones*, the only shrub that grows in those desolate *páramos*, trying unsuccessfully to make out what was happening.

It was about four o'clock when the sun broke through for a few minutes, just long enough for us to behold a scene of unequaled barbarity.

Some two hundred yards ahead of us eight *bandoleros*, in two groups, were tying ropes to the limbs of two completely naked young girls. The monsters were obviously intent on satisfying their crude carnal appetites, and the poor girls were struggling to keep them from consummating this outrage. Four of the *bandoleros* pulled hard on the ropes so that the violation would be all the more heinous, while two others acted as lookouts. The girls' cries for help were almost drowned out by the fury of the wind.

The *bandoleros* were dressed as our soldiers were, in khakis and ponchos.

We had to act quickly, but without risking the entire patrol, for there might be additional *bandoleros* hiding nearby.

At my command, the squad advanced in semicircle and opened fire. Six *bandoleros* fell dead at the feet of the girls, who now were weeping from the cold, and from shame and fright, and the two lookouts fled. Near the six dead bodies were shotguns, sharp machetes, and a .22 caliber pistol. I ordered my men to give the girls ponchos with which to cover themselves, since we could not find their clothes anywhere. One of the girls had been wounded in the hand when we opened fire on their attackers.

Having regained a little of their composure after those events, the girls told us what had happened. On Wednesday of Holy Week, in the afternoon, they had gone to confession at church in Ibagué; at five o'clock the next morning they were on their way to mass. But before they reached the church four *bandoleros* had seized them and taken them by car eastward at a high rate of speed. At some distance from the city they had met four more *bandoleros* waiting with mules. Gagged and securely bound, the girls were thrust into sacks and loaded onto the mules. On passing through military check point, they heard this curious dialogue:

"What do you have there?"

"Seed potatoes to plant."

"All right, go on."

The reader already knows the rest of the story.

The girls asked me to take them to Ibagué, where their parents were doubtless beside themselves with worry and distraught over their absence.

That night we slept in the woods, if it can be called sleeping. We lay still, half-frozen, listening to the wind whistling, with no protection other than our ponchos, and with nothing to eat but some *panela*.

At four in the morning on Good Friday we continued our march toward Juntas, taking proper security measures. We had gone about a mile when the *bandoleros* attacked, but swift action by our advance party cleared the road of the enemy. Two of them were killed, and we recovered for the military forces two Mauser rifles and a good supply of ammunition.

By one in the afternoon we were in Juntas, where the officers put a truck at our disposal, and we were able to continue on to Ibagué.

Having arrived at this city on the Combeima River, I got down from the truck and asked the owner of a general store whether he was Don Guillermo X.

"At your service," he replied. "What can I do for you?"

"Did you have two daughters kidnapped?"

"Why do you ask me that?"

"Oh, nothing; I was just asking, that's all."

"Man, my daughters are gone. Please, don't torment me. My wife is almost crazy with worry."

"Then, Don Guillermo, bring some clothes so they can dress, because I'm bringing your daughters back. They're out in the truck."

The old man, bursting with joy, went upstairs to tell his wife the good news. The parents could not thank us enough, and they simply forced us to accept blankets, cigarettes, and food.

We reported to the Roock Battalion and in army trucks, accompanied by Don Guillermo, we returned to Juntas, where the good man, not content with all he had done, rented mules to carry the things he had given us.

One of the Roock platoons escorted us to the scene of Thursday's action. The captain congratulated us and the lieutenant, on receiving the full account, ordered us back to La Paloma.

All the soldiers who patrolled with me during Holy Week were given several days' furlough—a fine reward whose value can only be appreciated by those who have put on the military uniform.*

I wish to pay special tribute in these pages to the outstanding performance of the soldiers from Chocó and Antioquia, who on that and on many other occasions brought great credit to their departments. We Colombians ought to be proud of the valor of our soldiers.** Our liberators did not exaggerate when they exalted the conduct of our soldier forebears

In recognition of the merits of my comrades-in-arms, I had wanted to write a work entitled "Nameless Heroes," as a

---

*After the Battle of Ayacucho, when Peru and Bolivia became independent, the colonel of the Army of Liberation, Francis Budett O'Connor, an Irishman, requested, as the only recompense for his services, permission to travel from Chuquisaca to Buenos Aires.

**Colombian and Venezuelan soldiers fought side by side against the Spanish, both on our soil and on the soil of our neighbor brothers. Speaking of our soldiers, Morillo wrote: "Fourteen successive charges against our tired battalions made me see that those men were not a little gang of weaklings, as I had been informed, but rather organized troops who could rival the King's best." Colonel O'Leary himself, speaking of the contingents of the liberating army that crossed the Andes, affirmed that South America did not have any better infantry soldiers than the brave men of the *Altiplano*.

tribute to their admirably anonymous but always brave performance; the title would have been most appropriate. A somewhat different book has taken precedence, however, and it warrants a different title.

11 · In Western Caldas

Hear counsel, and receive instruction, that thou mayest be wise in thy latter end. —Proverbs 19:20

I stayed for three months at Salento, in Caldas, as an assistant squad leader in the unit commanded by Captain Z.Z.

An assistant must possess qualities that enable him to command when the leader is absent, or to help the latter at any time. He must not be lacking in boldness, cleverness, decision, and certainly not in initiative.

A well-commanded squad can carry out difficult missions with success, since, as the regulations say, it is the smallest combat unit that combines firepower and movement.

Returning to Salento one day, at a place called Peña de la Virgen, we killed three dangerous *bandoleros*.

We were once more in Pereira when news reached the San Mateo Battalion that the *alcalde* of Apía had been murdered. Although the western part of the department of Caldas is rich and picturesque, the bellicosity of its inhabitants is even more pronounced. "Each one is as God made him, and sometimes, worse," as Sancho Panza slyly put it.

Allow me to digress for a moment. In 1949, on the occasion of the visit of national leaders of the Liberal Party to Río Sucio, there was a clash with dynamite and stones between the reds and the blues.† As the residents were return-

---

†Red and blue are the colors, respectively, of the Liberal and Conservative parties.

ing to their homes following this political demonstration, a revolver shot killed a nineteen-year-old youth.

A group from Supía came to claim the youth's body, but the peculiar thing about this sad case is that the town was divided: some were certain that the slain youth had been a Conservative, but those of the opposite party were equally certain that he had been a Liberal. Had not an army platoon been sent quickly from Río Sucio there would have been a fearful donnybrook in that mining town!

At eight o'clock that same evening, at an outlying cluster of houses, a powerful dynamite bomb exploded in a truck full of demonstrators. The consequences can easily be imagined—horribly mutilated limbs, gravely wounded people waiting hopelessly to be transported to the nearest hospital. Those who had been in the truck had not the slightest doubt that their political enemies had deliberately hurled the bomb into the vehicle as it approached the village. For the magistrate and his supporters the explanation was simple: the people in the truck were carrying the bomb, intending to throw it as they went through the town, but as luck would have it the device expoded before it was supposed to. You, dear reader, find the truth and arrest those responsible!

Such incidents were typical and frequent in our sadly notorious "first *violencia*."†

The murder of the *alcalde* of Apía alarmed the region. The government of Caldas named Lieutenant M.M. to execute the duties of the vacant office. I traveled with Sergeant 2nd Class X.X., as commander of the one of the squads of the platoon he commanded.

There were no police in Apía because any lawman who showed up there was a dead lawman. This was an extremely recalcitrant town, and to calm things down we had to exercise great patience. At the same time, we also had to demonstrate our firm dedication to the spirit and the letter of our watchword: 'Justice for all."

---

†Buitrago's historical flashback here is an accurate portrayal of a typical incident of Phase II in *la violencia*.

I always patrolled with Sergeant X.X., a noncom well experienced in maintaining public order. He gave me so much and such good advice that I do not hesitate to state that I owe to him a great part of my success in fighting the *bandoleros*.

"Listen to advice and you'll live to be an old man." If every soldier heeded this old saying, how many headaches and how much blood he would spare the army!

I stayed in Apía for thirteen months, during which time peace was established there. The Scripture says it is not good for man to live alone, and so on September 14, 1958, after obtaining the permission of my superiors—the army way—I received the nuptial blessing in Pereira.

12 · Traffic in Arms

Be suspicious and you will be right.

When I was promoted to the grade of Corporal 1st Class, in command of eighteen soldiers, they sent me as commander of the military post at Balboa, in the Department of Caldas.

The region was being scourged by the cruel acts of a *bandolero* nicknamed "Fosforito." The efforts of the police to capture him had been in vain. Every day the number of rural folk killed by the madness of this *bandolero* grew. I resolved to find out all I could about him and study his methods. I set an ambush for him and after a week I was successful in killing him. Higher echelons then decided to make the military post a more important installation and Lieutenant R. R. was put in command.

Toward the end of 1959 I was sent to La Virginia, where Captain T.T. assigned me to the detachment on the other side of the bridge over the Cauca River. My duty was to inspect two or three vehicles out of every ten that passed, because

the state of health of public order might be described as
"under the weather."

At three o'clock one Sunday afternoon I asked the driver
of a light truck for his papers. The man's reaction made me
suspicious. Quickly, I opened the door of the cab and got in.
Leaving the second-in-command in charge of the detachment,
I ordered the driver to cross the bridge and take me to the
army barracks.

The fellow answered me arrogantly and a little too excitedly. I shoved the muzzle of my carbine into his ribs and
ordered him to do as I had said.

When we stopped at an intersection, the driver made an
uproar to attract attention and demanded that I get out of
the truck. A crowd was gathering and the driver was gesticu-
lating and uttering threats, telling the crowd that the military
was abusing the civilians just because we wore uniforms.†
More and more spectators arrived and they were being persuaded by the loudly proclaimed innocence of my suspect.

Note the diabolical technique, certainly in wide use by
the communists, which consists of turning one's own guilt
against the guardians of order, whether they be the military,
the church, or the civil authorities.

Since in peace or war, nothing angers civilians more than
the searching of vehicles, the opportunity handed to the
driver was made to order. Taking advantage of the disorder of
the crowd, he fled.

Fortunately a local security patrol happened along, and
with its help I dispersed the crowd. Since I know how to
drive—this is something every soldier ought to be able to do—
I put the patrol on the truck, took the wheel, and drove on
to the barracks.

On examining the four big clay jars in the truck we found
that they were filled with oil. I did not feel satisfied about
the flight of the driver, however, so I shook the jars. Some-

---

†The department of Caldas was one of several that remained under
martial law (usually called *estado de sitio*, state of siege) throughout the
presidency of Dr. Alberto Lleras Camargo.

thing metallic hit the sides and we realized that the jars did not seem to weigh as much as they should. Turning them upside down, we found that each jar had a false bottom ingeniously sealed inside. We broke them open and found nine .22 caliber carbines and five thousand rounds of ammunition.

In the military, and even more where public order is involved, the proverb is confirmed: Be suspicious and you will be right!

Though apparently more useful in sport than in war, carbines, with their range, their accuracy, and the fact that they make little noise, have caused many a casualty in our ranks.

13 · El Puntudo

The sword serves justice and defends the law.

"El Puntudo" was a dangerous *bandolero* who operated for a long time in the Cañon de Totuí region, within the jurisdiction of the town of Balboa in Caldas.

This criminal was a recluse who performed his misdeeds alone, but he was responsible for many deaths. Besides the little people slain by his bloody machete and the dumdum bullets of his carbine, El Puntudo had killed the police inspector of Totuí, two *carabineros* (mounted troops of the National Police), and a policeman in Santuario, another town in the department of Caldas.

This one-man gang was a strange case, a misbegotten fiend, who prowled those fertile lands as if they were his own, and acting as if he were lord and master of haciendas and of lives.

From 4th Brigade headquarters in Medellín came orders to find El Puntudo and bring him in, dead or alive.

I was under the command of Captain T.T., commander of the Public Order Battery with headquarters in La Virginia. He was a very serious officer, overly meticulous, one might say, but an excellent commander and very good to his subordinates.

With the proper authorization from headquarters, two *carabineros* from Caldas and I entered the Cañon del Totuí in search of the criminal, El Puntudo.

For several days we patrolled a part of the canyon called Llano Grande. My companions could not have been better—brave, enterprising, attentive, and, on occasion, daring.

On the fourth day of our search we met up with this enemy of society, of whom a description would be of interest before continuing the account.

El Puntudo was rather short and thin, with a cone-shaped head and a prominent nose—peculiarities to which he owed his sobriquet *"puntudo"* (pointed, pointy, full of points). He was olive-skinned and had wavy hair with long sideburns, and, to top it all off, he was almost blind in one eye, which was clouded and made him appear terribly ugly. He wore a khaki shirt and trousers, a black *ruana* and coffee-colored *guayos*. He carried a two-edged machete stuck in a leather sheath adorned with filigree, and he was never without his two revolvers and his 22.-caliber carbine. His thin, squeaky voice made him even more disagreeable and repulsive. He was twenty-four years old and a native of Balboa.

In these *bandolero* activities one-eyed people have the reputation of being *"pícaros,"* a term that the people have continued to apply to every one-eyed person. They say that near Yopal, in Casanare, "Tuerto" (one-eyed) Giraldo actively fought against the police and that he surrendered his weapons shortly after the events of the thirteenth of June, 1953.†

In Carare and in the south of the department of Magdalena there was a "Corporal Chicote," also a one-eyed man, dark and slight; they say he was "helped" or "protected," because in frequent encounters with the troops the latter's

---

†The reference is to the overthrow of President Laureano Gómez by General Gustavo Rojas Pinilla.

bullets bounced off his belt buckle without causing him the least harm. He also surrendered.

But let me resume the account of our dealings with El Puntudo.

"Show me your papers," the little man ordered us point blank.

"Certainly, here they are," we replied, holding out before his piercing gaze the documents that accredited us as authentic *bandoleros*.

While El Puntudo seemed to be studying these written testimonials, one of the *carabineros*, from Antioquia, with that gift and facility for lying some of the *antioqueños* have, was boasting about us.

"To test you," said El Puntudo, "We'll do a simple little job. We'll kill the mayor of Santuario. He's a Liberal."

We were three to one, and it might have been possible for us to subdue this fellow, swaggering around with his weapons. However, since this man had so many entries in the local crime reports, it was necessary to check out his contacts and any arms caches he might have.

We determined, therefore, to go along with him, and to grab him at the first opportunity.

Before reaching Santuario, in the meadows known as *las Savanitas*, we stopped to eat some oranges to satisfy our appreciable hunger and thirst. As one of the *carabineros*, perched up in the tree, was tossing us the best fruit, I remembered a story about *la violencia* in the *llanos* of Casanare, as recounted by soldiers who had experienced it: on many occasions solders had been killed by booby traps hidden in artificial oranges. I wondered whether El Puntado might not have prepared such a trap for us.

Something must have made the malefactor suspicious while we were busy eating the oranges, because on the pretext of going to relieve himself he started running for the dense woods.

The *carabineros*, however, had good hands they could use, and, being afraid such a criminal might go free to continue slaying innocent citizens at his whim, they opened fire at him.

We returned to the barracks, leaving to the local people
the burial of the body of the man who had been the scourge
of their region.

14 · Help!

Cobbler, to your last.

Officers and noncoms are subject to change of station as the
needs of the army dictate, and unless one has attained high
rank it is better not to put down roots because eventually,
roots and all, one will have to pack up, fill out forms, and arrange transportation to a new unit way off somewhere.

I was very satisfied in my work having to do with the
maintaining of public law and order; then in May 1959 orders
came down transferring me to the 5th Galán Artillery Battalion, quartered at Socorro.

Socorro is a distinguished city, conscious of its tradition
and full of history. In Socorro was born the "Comunero"
movement, one comparable in historic importance only to
that of Tupac Amaru in Peru.†

Its climate is pleasant, its markets are well stocked, and
its citizens are friendly toward strangers. The barracks had
not yet been completed, however, and this made life uncom-
fortable for the military personnel. I was an instructor in the
topography section. Garrison life was peaceful, but despite
the pleasantness of Socorro my wife became bored and so did
I. She missed the kind of food she was accustomed to back in
Caldas, and she missed her family; I remembered with a cer-

---

†Buitrago refers here to the Revolt of the *Comuneros*, 1781–82, in
which a huge, spontaneous uprising among the farmers and townsmen
swept through Santander and adjacent provinces. The revolt was put
down through a combination of viceregal treachery and brute force.

tain longing my days of patrolling in the region caught up in
la violencia—those patrols that quicken the emotions and
cause one to reflect on the importance of the military profession.

I wrote to Colonel P.P., who was then commanding officer of the San Mateo Battalion, asking his help [*socorro*]. He
in turn spoke to General S.S., and in November 1959 Corporal Buitrago was back in Pereira—which once again confirms
the Scriptural saying: Ask and it shall be given you!

I remained at Pereira for a year and a half, in charge of
the military police unit. I used this time to good advantage;
in addition to carrying out my sometimes tiresome duties in
pursuing and guarding deserters, helping the National Police
catch thieves and marijuana peddlers, cooperating with DAS
and F-2,† and so forth, I also did a lot of studying on my
own. I often read until dawn about the life of the cowboys of
the western United States and stories about the FBI, and
everything related to police and detective work.

Whenever they showed films about war or other things
related to my favorite reading topics, I was the first one
there—never missing a word, a gesture, or a move of the pro-
tagonists.

I can state that I learned many things from these readings
and movies that would prove very useful in my subsequent
activities on behalf of law and order.

How I envied those gunslingers on the screen—good guys
and bad—with their fast draws. If what was being flashed on
the screen was pure fiction, I was determined to make at least
some of it real. So it was a logical result of my readings and
the films that there I was, practicing shooting with the revolver, with right hand, left hand, from any position—imitat-
ing Bat Masterson.

I finally attained a dexterity and accuracy of which I am
quite proud. I made target practice a subject for dedicated

---

†DAS stands for Departamento Administrativo de Seguridad, the
Colombian equivalent of the FBI. F-2 is a special criminal-investigative
section of the National Police.

study. As will be evident later, this has served me well.

It may seem foolish, but it really is not, to recommend to every professional soldier a dedication to target practice with the revolver, the carbine, the rifle, the automatic rifle, shotgun, and other weapons. On the one hand, target practice prepares one for performing effectively in combat; on the other, this exercise should prepare him well for intraservice competitions in peacetime, and for matches with civilian gun clubs.

Whether taken as a sport or as part of service, marksmanship training enables a man to appreciate his own capabilities, to discipline himself, and to increase his self-confidence. When one has achieved a certain degree of proficiency in the handling of firearms, these instruments are appreciated in their full value as an extension of one's own strength and as an effective means of performing one's duty.

15 · Bearing the Cross

He who marries will want a house and a shopping bag.

On July 18, 1961, I returned to the San Mateo Battalion after six weeks in Bogotá, where I had completed the first course in intelligence training. Two days later a radiogram from the high command ordered my immediate assignment to the detachment in Armenia.

When transfers come one feels the full weight of the responsibility of matrimony. Civilians, fortunately for them, do not know what it really means to be transferred "immediately" or "in the shortest possible time" or "as soon as one can get there."

Once I arrived at the flourishing city of Armenia, following the old saying, "He who marries will want a house and a shopping bag," I set about combing the city in search of a place to live. No sooner had I found a place than I had to break the lease because I had been assigned to the detachment in Zarzal, in the northern part of Valle.

They talked of Zarzal being "out of order." That is, there was little law and order in the region, which was infested with antisocial types and men of violence. In the garrison guardhouse were some forty "suspects" and prisoners. There were also many informants, civilians familiar with the gangs of *bandoleros* and their haunts. These informants collaborated with the authorities, either for a stipend or in consideration of other, sometimes significant, rewards.

Information, information! Only on the basis of information can success in warfare—regular or guerrilla—be achieved. Obtain information, convert it into intelligence, and then take appropriate action. But never move blindly!

So there I was with the detachment in northern Valle, this time working with a sergeant 2nd class who was a specialist in interrogating prisoners. He was a good friend and an excellent noncom.

A skillful interrogation can shed much light on things. It is an art to be able to interrogate prisoners without violating the rules laid down in regulations and the constitutionally guaranteed civil rights. A word, a sound, a movement, a look from the suspect may lead to the clearing up of a massacre. The old saw: "Cleverness is better than force," applies to this technique perfectly; and also: "More flies are caught with a drop of honey than with a barrel of bile."

To be an interrogation specialist one must study every day and add to what one has already learned. Most civilians have no concept of the intensive and multifaceted activities of the military. They judge us by appearances; they see us parade on national holidays in eye-catching uniforms and are convinced that barracks life consists of marching to the music of a military band. How mistaken they are! To march, to parade, is one of the accessory activities, but not the fundamental one.

Modern warfare in its various ramifications—such as insurgency—demands constant preparation on the part of the soldier, not in just one branch of the science but in all. Today, in the barracks, one spends one's time studying, and one cannot be promoted without having passed a course of instruction. War is not only a clash of bodies but also of intelligences. The steady stream of military-trained professionals, technicians, and specialists, who, year after year, are returned to the ranks of civilian enterprise, gives an indication of the variety of studies and training carried out by the military. From the barracks come drivers, heavy-machinery operators, male nurses, telegraphers, electricians, electronic specialists, engineers—all with sound training received in the army. (The foregoing, of course, does not attempt to include all the specialists from the navy and the air force, because the list would be too long.) What we do in the barracks is to prepare ourselves physically and mentally for the decisive test: war. While we await that test, we study and we strengthen ourselves physically to serve in peace.

Well, dear reader, back to the account. I repeat, I had to leave my family and go to Zarzal. The honor of wearing the uniform imposes such renunciations.

16 · They've Killed Lieutenant Jaramillo!

Justice may limp along, but it does get there.

While I was in northern Valle we heard the news of the murder of the military mayor of Ansermanuevo, Lieutenant Rudecindo Jaramillo.

There was surprise, indignation, recollections, exclamations, and a great bustling at our headquarters. Radiograms were received and sent and couriers left and returned with communiques and classified documents.

An immediate drive was being mounted to locate those responsible. Not for nothing had we had intelligence training!

An informant told us that in Bugalagrande he had seen a "suspicious looking" man who was hiding out around there and avoiding people who passed by. To work! As they say: "Time is money" and "Heaven helps the man who gets up early."

Together with the informant and Sergeant L.L., I went to Bugalagrande. For six hours, we reconnoitered the area around the house that the informant pointed out to us and finally located the mystery man. Calmly, as if we were just traveling along the road, we moved toward the house. I went to ask for a drink of water while my companion, the sergeant, covered the front door. A man greeted me in friendly fashion, but I knew that the man we were looking for was watching me from behind a curtain. I noticed some papayas on the patio and asked the man who gave me water if he would sell me some of the fruit. He replied affirmatively, whereupon I darted through the kitchen and ran outside. Quickly I stuck my gun through a window and pointed it at the man inside. I had moved so fast that he still had his back to me. With my revolver aimed at him, I said, "Don't move! Now, raise your hands!"

My move was backed up by the vigilant sergeant, who, as I said, had stayed at the entrance of the house. Coordination, common sense, cleverness, and quickness had put this dangerous thug into my custody. Nicknamed "Palizada," this monster, whose photo we were carrying in order to identify him, had directed the murder of Lieutenant Jaramillo.

Why had they killed Jaramillo in 1962? Because, as an honorable soldier, he had carried out his responsibilities without political discrimination. For that reason, for being just, for doing his duty as a soldier, for not showing favoritism, they had murdered him. My readers should be startled. It was learned that a lady by the name of G.C., the leader of one of the Conservative Party organizations in Ansermanuevo, had paid twenty-five thousand pesos to have Jaramillo killed.

Palizada confessed: he and three others had killed the military mayor. The sergeant and I turned him over to the judge and went in search of the three remaining criminals, who reportedly were hiding out around Roble.

Despite all our efforts and diligence we never caught up with them. Three months later, however, they were shot down by our troops.

17 · It's Important to Keep Count!

In counterguerrilla operations a series of partial successes leads to definitive victory.

One day they gave us the assignment of capturing a *bandolero*, whose name escapes me but who had been seen walking around brazenly on the streets of Zarza. We already knew distinctive characteristics of his appearance, so the sergeant and I resolutely set out for Zarza.

It was night when we went out to check the town, or as we say in Pereira, to take a stroll around. As we moved along a little-traveled street, we saw a man leaning against the door of a barber shop. Just in case this might be our man, we decided to ask him for his identification. The fellow replied with two revolver shots that, fortunately for us, missed. With a leap, the gunman burst into the barber shop and shielded himself behind one of the barber chairs. We exchanged fire—a dangerous game, and that fellow was mean. But as we fired I was keeping track of his shots: three, four, five, six. Once sure that my enemy had no shots left, I rushed in with the intention of capturing him.

Instead of surrendering he rushed at me and would have killed me with a knife or a blow if an accurate shot had not dropped him dead on the spot.

"War is not waged for the love of God," said Bolívar in 1824, when he was preparing to destroy Spain's rule forever.

When the authorities made their routine examination of the body they confirmed that he had been one of the criminal participants in the ambush of an army squad at Germania, near Cartago. The patrol had been traveling in a military truck, unfortunately without an escort and therefore in violation of the principle of security.* At a curve in the road, the truck was hit with rifle fire and hand grenades. The sergeant in command, riding in the cab, was picked off before he could issue a single order. Four soldiers died in the back of the truck, horribly mangled by the grenades. Another fell from the vehicle and was butchered by the villains, who rifled the body after cutting off the head and tossing it into the bushes. In defiance of the military, the attackers left on the mutilated body cards bearing the names and photographs of several of the savage assailants!

I forgot to say that the others in the patrol had been wounded or rendered unconscious as a result of the explosions and thus were incapable of reacting and making use of their weapons. The driver, however, in an act of outstanding bravery, had thrown the truck into reverse and backed up with the accelerator to the floorboard; then he slammed on the brakes and scrambled to the back of the truck, where he seized an automatic rifle and fired a long burst at the *bandoleros*. Then he took the wheel again and managed to drive off, bringing the wounded to the Sagrado Corazón de Jesús Hospital in Cartago and thereby saving their lives.

Let this be a word of praise for the conduct of civilian personnel serving the Ministry of Defense (formerly the Ministry of War). These people have shared our anguish and our success in the long and violent struggle against the *bandoleros*.

The funeral chamber at the Vencedores Battalion was filled with candles and flowers, black armbands and weeping. The blood-streaked arms of the crucified Christ spread compassionately over six caskets, each draped lovingly with the flag of Colombia.

---

*Security: this is the protection against espionage, sabotage, observation, infiltration, or surprise attack by the enemy, preventing him from interfering with our freedom of action.

18 · How Much Are Carbines?

Weapons? The Enemy's.

In 1962 the detachment was moved from Zarzal to Cartago. I was part of the Mobile Intelligence Group, and the commander put a jeep at my disposal. Assignments were given to us and we were allowed ample—even unlimited—time to carry them out. Our officers had absolute confidence in us. Mental alertness, physical strength, determination, and the firm conviction that one acts in a just cause are qualities inherent in soldiers selected for this special work.†

No vices! The worst enemy of the soldier, in peace or war, is alcohol! And women, to be with them and not become involved! One who is not capable of overcoming the twin temptations of alcohol and women will fail sooner or later. And another thing—the soldier must have an aptitude for playing any role his assignment may require.

Once I was in Cartago dressed as a civilian, with sideburns and long hair, and, apparently because my unkempt appearance inspired their confidence, some fellows offered to sell me some homemade .38-caliber, long-rifle carbines, Craftily, I told them I needed three. They agreed to get them for me.

When I met them again two weeks later, they told me they had only two guns. I asked that we go somewhere and test them. We went along the road that runs between Cartago and Pereira and turned off at a certain spot and crossed a field. They showed me a carbine and demanded six hundred pesos for each weapon. I said I wanted to try them personally, since I was the one who would use them. They replied that they didn't have any ammunition. I was carrying some with me, so I took a gun, put eight cartridges in the magazine,

---

†This assignment was Buitrago's introduction to the bandit-infiltration program, in which several dozen skilled noncoms were given broad latitude to identify, infiltrate, and eliminate the leadership structure of the bandit gangs.

and took aim at a distant target. Then, wheeling around to my suppliers, I ordered, "Hands up!" One of them, who had a cut on his face, tried to draw his pistol, but I was faster: I fired and wounded him in the leg. I disarmed them both and made the uninjured one carry his wounded companion to my car. Having tied them both up, hand and foot, with some electric-light cord, I drove them to Cartago and turned them over to the DAS, whose agents then took the wounded man to the hospital.

Thus was uncovered a clandestine arms factory that produced automatic carbine with magazines holding thirty rounds and with good range and better accuracy.

You see, we are not so "underdeveloped" . . .

19 · A Good Fright

Man proposes and God disposes.

If you, as a good *carabinero* of the National Police, notice that a suspicious looking person is boarding a train, you will, in sound logic, proceed to search him. If said suspect turns out to be armed to the teeth with two .38-caliber revolvers and a belt full of cartridges, in the style of Juan Charrasquiado, you have no choice, as a good police officer, than to arrest him, take him to headquarters, and interrogate him.

Furthermore, if all this happens a few hours after a killing in a zone frequented by the *bandoleros*, the suspect has to consider himself lucky if he preserves his physical integrity. These are things of *la violencia.* What else are we to do!

Well, then, this was what happened to me when I was about to get on the train in Alcalá. What an appearance I must have made when I attracted the attention of the police.

The acting sergeant, a very energetic man, questioned me. I replied, seemingly calm, saying I was a worker, from one of my own *fincas*, and that I was carrying the weapons for my personal safety.

The story was not convincing, apparently, because they took me out in the middle of the night to a *cafetal* at the edge of Alcalá and said they would kill me if I did not "come clean."

"All right now, tell us, without any more fooling around, who are you?"

The success of the work of the Mobile Intelligence Group vitally depends on our not being identified. For that reason I wanted to remain silent.

"Tell us if you are a secret agent and that will be that. Don't make us waste time."

"If you are a member of a gang and you want to save your skin and get a reward besides, tell us where your buddies are."

I tried to bribe the sergeant by offering him the attractive sum of a thousand pesos. Horrors! I should never have said it! So mistaken was my proposal, and such was the indignation of the sergeant, that to save my life I pulled out (of my left shoe) my identification papers.

The zealous police were still doubtful, however, because the next day they led me, well guarded, to the military post at Alcalá, where an army noncom returned to me my honor, my revolvers, and my ammunition.

20 · One More for Conrado's Gang

He who wants to kiss looks for the mouth.

The region of the Quindío was held under the scourge of the gang of Conrado Salazar, alias Zarpazo. Murders, robberies, threats, extortions (*boletos*),* all occurred continually at the direction of this *bandolero*. Among his evil deeds was the massacre in 1962 at Cayetana, in which he killed thirty-one persons.

I proposed to an informant, X, who enjoyed the high confidence of the commander of our detachment and was, as well, a contact with Zarpazo's band, that he take me to his *finca*. After reflecting on it, the man agreed to do so, adding that it would be a magnificent opportunity for me to become acquainted with the gang's territory.

It was my intention to infiltrate Zarpazo's gang, working, of course, with the proper authorization of my superiors. The task was risky, but if I managed to carry it off society and the army would benefit greatly, because I hoped to destroy the beast in his own den.

Before undertaking such a dangerous job, in which I certainly would be risking my life, I went to Pereira and explained to my wife that they had ordered me on a mission that would last two or three months, and that I would be in charrge of a post in the mountains. Also, I asked her to pray that nothing happened to me.

The informan's *finca* was situated above Albania, where in 1962 the *bandoleros* had killed a sergeant 2nd class and five soldiers. The trip by car from Cartago to the hacienda took half an hour. I carried a suitcase with a few clothes and some books so that the *bandoleros* would think I was a student.

---

*Boleteos. "Through the system called and generally known by the name *boleteo*, one demanded from the owners of *fincas* and *haciendas* large sums of money to be delivered within a fixed time, under the threat of losing life and property.

"Many owners of *fincas* and *haciendas*, having lost faith and confidence in the authorities and fearing the reprisals of the *bandoleros*, preferred to pay the large sums of money and keep silent." Taken from *De la violencia a la paz.* [A special report, well documented, by the 8th Army Brigade on its intensive and original anti-*violencia* operations in the department of Caldas.]

The day after our arrival Conrado Salazar appeared with twenty-two men armed with rifles, San Cristobal carbines, revolvers, and MK-2 grenades.

Conrado asked X who I was and the informant told him I was no less than his nephew, a law student at Manizales, who was enjoying a few days vacation.

The ruse, prepared by X and me, worked. I was on one of the porches of the house when Conrado and Tista Tabares approached me in a very friendly manner and asked me about life in Manizales.

Seated on a large bench Conrado showed me a Bereta submachine gun, which certainly did not come from our military forces. He let me look at it for a while and then asked:

"Do you like it?"

"Sure," I answered.

"I'll sell it to you," said Conrado.

"I don't have any money," I replied. "Besides, what would I want with that?"

"You know anything about rifles and carbines?" he asked.

"I'm in the reserves," I answered, so he would not catch me in a lie if later I carelessly said something revealing.

He let me hold the gun for a few minutes more and then said, point blank, "If you're a reservist, you'll make a good lookout."

With that he handed me a pair of binoculars and pointed out the places along which any approaching troops would have to pass.

Since I was standing guard, the twenty-two *bandoleros* and their chief sat down to lunch on the patio.

What a marvelous opportunity was being offered me to kill this Conrado and decimate his gang! If I could shoot this submachine gun, I was thinking, I could kill quite a few, and then I could escape and return to the detachment. But the wily Zarpazo had not shown me how to use the weapon. If I tried to fire and failed, they would kill me on the spot, with no benefit to the armed forces.

At about three in the afternoon, I sighted a mounted army patrol, perhaps a squad, headed for where we were. It was coming from a place called Carbonera. "Here come the *chulos!*" I shouted, with all the force of my lungs. Instantly, the gang took headlong flight.

Twenty minutes later the soldiers were searching the house. They asked me for papers and I showed them my citizenship papers, a military ID card, and a student card, without identifying myself as a noncom.

After the soldiers had left, the informant, X, asked me about my having given the warning to Salazar.

If I had not done as I had, the gang would have annihilated the patrol, which had been moving along the road bunched together, without security distance—a very common and often-disastrous error. In guerrilla warfare, such mistakes in movement and execution are paid for in blood. My conscience was clear. On the one hand, I had saved the lives of my companions in arms. On the other, I had gained the confidence of Conrado, who considered the warning an unmistakeable sign of my loyalty.

The day after this incident, Conrado returned to the *finca*, gave me an *abrazo*, and told me I was a good fellow and worthy of his absolute confidence.

"You've got the nerve and the steadiness it takes to make a good *guerrillero*," he said. "Give up that studying and come with me. Studying law is no real business. Spending your time getting rowdies out of jail doesn't pay. Here in the woods you make a few bucks. I promise to treat· you right. Make up your mind; I'll be back day after tomorrow."

This was almost too much! That he should say this to me! I said I would think about it, but I had already decided to go with him.

I did not tell the informant anything about this for fear he might betray me. I just behaved normally, and on Thursday, when Conrado Salazar appeared, I told my pretended uncle I was going to Cartago to get some clothes, and told Zarpazo, in private, "I'm going with you. I lied to my uncle; I told him I was going back to town to study today."

"That's fine that way," Conrado replied. "Now, go on down the road and where you see a big *yarumo* on the right, turn off there without leaving any tracks; go down the *cafetal*, go straight ahead and you'll find a big tree."

Twenty-four years old, short, heavy-set, with a dark, Indian face, a bit cross-eyed, with two birthmarks on his left cheek and a big machete scar on the back of his neck—this Conrado, who could read a little but could not write, was giving me his first order. The die was cast. Come what might, I had faith in God, and I believed in my own ability.

21 · Extortion and Bivouac

Man is wolf to man.   —Plautus

Near a *zurrumbo* tree five *bandoleros* and two women were waiting. I did not know any of them but they, when they saw me, exclaimed: "Hello, Mono. So you finally made up your mind, huh?"

Half an hour later, Conrado and the rest of the gang joined us.

"Are you afraid?" he asked me.

"I have to die some day one way or another," I replied. "If it's going to be the soldiers that kill me, why what the Hell, let them kill me!"

This was good straight talk in front of my new companions-to-be, who commented among themselves: "There's a real man!"

Avoiding roads and trails, in good *bandolero* fashion, we climbed the steep cordillera for an hour. At a certain spot in a woods, six workers from a nearby hacienda appeared with six big pots containing food. The logistics worked precisely when the *chulos* were far away.

A good lunch calls for a good siesta. For that reason, and also because in war a soldier ought to be a meal and a night's sleep ahead, Conrado, after posting lookouts, ordered us to rest on the ground on our ponchos (*ruanas*) in broad daylight. It was eight in the evening when we left that place and headed for the settlement of Morro Azul.

Night marches afford protection from observation and make it possible to withdraw from positions that are in danger of being discovered. The *bandolero* cannot settle down anywhere, since his security and the success of his missions depend in part on his mobility.

We spent two weeks in the shelter of the stalks of a huge clump of bamboo, sleeping on bamboo pallets, and slipping down to the Vieja River every other day, to bathe or to fish.

The local inhabitants who happened to see us never opened their mouths, following an old saying that is a norm and a guide for the weak and the pusillanimous: If you want to enjoy this life, look, listen, and keep your mouth shut!

The food was plentiful and served on time. It was prepared in the house of Gerardo Cardona, a *mayordomo* of a neighboring *finca*.* Conrado paid out the money, and Don Gerardo carried out his duties to the fullest.

Zarpazo exacted "taxes" from the owners of haciendas in the region by means of *boletos* such as this: "Don 'Zutanito,' you are to send with the bearer two thousand pesos."

Fear of reprisals from the gang brought money pouring in for the chief's purse. So far as money was concerned, he was not wrong when he advised me to abandon the study of law and come to the hills with him.

Since the zone in which we were operating was extensive, any one hacienda owner would get an extortion note only once or twice a year. But the contributions did not stop there, because of that part of the coffee that properly be-

---

*The *mayordomo, agregado,* or administrator of a *finca* was a key figure in this matter of *la violencia* in the Quindío. Sometimes he would become the virtual owner, and the harvest would be divided among the *bandolero* chief, the administrator, and the true owner.

longed to the administrator at the harvest, the administrator had to give Conrado a tenth plus the first fruits.

The coffee was left with Cardona, who was responsible for selling it for Conrado. Sometimes the extortion note demanded no less than ten thousand pesos from the chosen victim; the latter, mustering all the courage he could, might come through with five thousand, an amount that might for a while satisfy the enormous greed of my new commander.

With the money collected by his strong-arm technique Conrado bought clothing for his men, and lanterns, batteries, etc., and sometimes paid for the food that was supplied.

Every two weeks he gave five of his men a "pass," selecting those who were the least known to the local authorities. He gave each man three hundred pesos so he could get something to drink, have a spree, and get a woman.

I told Conrado that he shouldn't let his people go to town because they might betray us at any moment, and he should remember that he had quite a price on his head.

"Not at all," he replied. "You have to let them have a good time. If you don't want to go, don't."

And so it was, over the months and the years: the hacienda owners of the Quindío paid tribute to *la violencia*. Their honest labor, the bread for their children, the harvest of their good land, tilled with love and watered by their sweat all year—all this would end up in the war chest of a *bandolero*, a bandit chief, a "hero worthy of emulation" according to some of my misguided compatriots.†

---

†Buitrago's bitter inference stems from the fact that the National *Violencia* Investigatory Commission concluded that many *bandoleros* were victims of the social system, and the fact that certain researchers did indeed write political tracts featuring individual bandits as folk heroes. A primary example is Monsignor Germán Guzmán, who supported the notorious Teófilo Rojas ("Chispas") as a true fighter for justice, an interpretation highly colored by the monsignor's role as a left-wing political activist.

22 · Twenty-Four Minus Five is Nineteen

For grave ills, drastic remedies.

Several weeks had passed since my joining Conrado Salazar's band, and I had been taking advantage of the time to study the habits, the combat procedures, and the nature of my companions-through-circumstance.

Now it was time to take some action against these men, who scoffed at laws and rights as they massacred, robbed, and collected extortion money. I was between a rock and a hard place. If I met up with army troops, I could not identify myself to them. If I did nothing and compliantly went along with the gang, I would be unworthy of the trust that the brigade had placed in me, and I would be untrue to my own resolve. Something had to be done at once, and I made ready to do it.

We were camped near the Cañón del Sende when the troops moved against us in an *"operación del berriondo,"* as Tista Tabares called it—like the charge of an enraged animal.

I was sent with two others to serve as scouts to observe the troop's movements. Conrado, Tista, and the rest stayed back some five hundred yards.

The soldiers were coming closer. Contact was imminent. I ordered the two *bandoleros* to climb an avocado tree so they could see better, but I really had something else in mind. I stayed on the ground and released the safety of my weapon. (All three of us carried San Cristóbal carbines.)

It must have been about six in the afternoon when I heard several detonations from below our position. The troopers had formed a skirmish line; now was my chance.

As the men in the tree took aim at the soldiers at almost point-blank range, I raised my carbine toward the foliage and fired. The two fell from the tree like ripe avocados.

I dashed back to where Conrado was without bothering

to take the weapons from the dead men, because the army would do that in good time.

Conrado, however, and his men were on the run, too; the troopers had killed one of his men. I had to rejoin the gang at once. To delay would simply be to condemn myself. On skirting a canebreak I unexpectedly met up with a *bandolero* straggler. With a shot to his head I left him dead and kept running, leaving his gun with him.

At about three in the morning, after a peril-filled night spent in dizzying flight from the pursuit of the soldiers, we stopped at the place called Las Coloradas. When daylight came, Conrado checked over his men; nine were missing, but at noon five who had become separated rejoined us.

The gang had four transistor radios, which were turned on, and we heard the following news item: "In a clash with the gang of Conrado Salazar, four of the *bandoleros* were killed, and one Mauser rifle and two San Cristóbal carbines were recovered."

I noticed that one of the men had evidently thrown away his weapon in the flight. I slyly brought this fact to Conrado's attention. "A *guerrillero* should never be separated from his weapon for any reason in the world," I told him. "Better to be killed than separated from your gun. That guy's no good to us at all!"

Conrado asked a few questions and then ordered his erstwhile follower out of camp.

In Machiavellian fashion, I approached Tista Tabares and murmured into his ear: "Man, that guy is going to tell the troops where we are. It would be better to get rid of him!"

Tista, the second in command, or as one might say, Conrado's executive officer, ordered two of his henchmen to "execute the command."

The day's work had been profitable. Of twenty-four *bandoleros* only nineteen were left.

In guerrilla warfare as waged in the Quindío highlands I could do nothing except respond to violence with violence. Consequently applying Machievelli's maxim, "divide and conquer," I caused these very *bandoleros* to begin their mutual elimination. My life hung by a thread, because there began to be some murmurings among the *bandoleros*, and it was possible that Zarpazo might become suspicious. But, gut it out, and fight fire with fire, as they say back home; my assigned mission was being carried out, and it was necessary to carry it to its conclusion, cost what it might.

At dusk, as light was giving way to darkness, in those moments when day and night mix and souls are filled with boundless nostalgia, I seemed to see in the clouds, rosy rimmed by the sun's last rays, the faces of my daughters far away. Yearning for my distant home, with the spotless table attended with love and affection, the simple things that give warmth to family life, the prayers with which one calls on God each day—how I longed to be able to bridge the distance in an instant and once more be a part of the pleasant life of the city. But then an order from Conrado, a growl from Tista Tabares, a movement of the sentinels, or the signal flashed from a distant light, announcing the presence of the troops, brought me back to reality. From the depths of my being came a Biblical verse that gave me courage: "Work and be expectant."

23 · Cryptography

There is nothing new under the sun.

Tista Tabares was falling-down drunk; his bloodshot eyes showed his state of intoxication.

The past few days of relative calm had given the gang a breathing spell. We were split up: Conrado was over near Morro Azul; Corporal Ochoa was at Las Coloradas; and at the house of a brother of Gerardo Gallego were Tabares, Gata, and the author of these memoirs.

We were so few that we could not afford the luxury of

posting a guard during the day. Even so, a diligent washwoman served as a lookout. The system was simple and ingenious: half a dozen pigs were allowed out of their pen to wander up toward the *cafetal* in search of worms to supplement their diet. If the woman smelled danger, she had only to call the pigs, as she customarily did, to give them water: "Chitooooó! Chitooooó!" The herd would hurry back at the call and we, properly warned, would hastily depart.

I ask you, what troops, however well trained and however suspicious, would decipher the simple call to the pigs as a warning to the enemy? How true it is that appearances deceive!

Trusting in our security system, Tista, that day, was having himself a party; everything in a *bandolero's* life cannot be hardship. And what a party! He was enjoying the caresses of a fiery fifteen-year-old girl and the bouquet of a liquor supplied by local vineyards.

However, since in this devilish world nothing is ever so good or so bad as it could be, all of a sudden there appeared a messenger who threatened to interrupt that moment of diversion. Tista was in no mood for messages and so, recovering from the first moment of surprise, in his booze-soaked voice he said to me: "Hey, Zarquito, decode this message Conrado sent."

"How the devil can I do that?" I asked.

"That's easy. Take the key and you'll see."

Then forgetting about the messenger and the rest of us, he brutishly returned to his amorous pursuits.

In my hand I held a piece of plan paper full of numbers written in pencil but with great care. Instantly I recalled seeing many such papers, to which I had paid no attenttion, when I was patrolling with the army in western Caldas. These were papers that *bandoleros* said were just an innocent record of their daily wages.

There is really nothing new under the sun, as was affirmed by the wise Israelite, the one with nine-hundred wives!

For if the regular army uses complicated keys, machines,

codes and substitutions, the *bandoleros* also devise their own secret writing system, no less effective just because it is rudimentary, as can be seen in the message I deciphered.*

45 - 31 - 47 - 31 - 46 - 31 - 35 - 48 - 45 - 40
46 - 38 - 48 - 31 - 43 - 31 - 52 - 46 - 54 - 36
55 - 36 - 35 - 36 - 43 - 31 - 46 - 48 - 34 - 36
46 - 48 - 52 - 36 - 46 - 33 - 48 - 46 - 53 - 51
31 - 45 - 48 - 52 - 36 - 46 - 43 - 31 - 37 - 40
46 - 33 - 31 - 36 - 43 - 40 - 46 - 37 - 40 - 36
51 - 46 - 48 - 59 - 31 - 51 - 49 - 31 - 59 - 48

(Tomorrow Sunday at 9:00 P.M. we meet at the *finca* El Infierno. Zarpazo.)

Later I learned that such encoded messages went from the *bandoleros* to the cities and vice versa. As a counterintelligence measure, in the answer the chief or the person involved would move the key one number to the right. At Tista's orders Machetazo—that was the messenger's nickname—ate lunch with us. The *sancocho* that day was particularly good, with nuggets of chicken fat floating in that sometimes "dangerous" concoction, a marvelous substance capable of reviving the dead or fortifying newlyweds. Gata said nothing; he helped his digestion by sharpening his machete with a triangular file until it had a razor edge on both sides—like the wife of an Antioquian barber, as they say.

Tista Tabares and his female companion, both exhausted by their gastronomic and carnal excesses, were sound asleep.

I exchanged a few monosyllables with Gata, and abruptly Machetazo departed, confirming the accuracy of the old saying: A fed Indian is a gone Indian! San Blas, now you've eaten, now you're leaving!

---

*The key to the code [in Spanish]:

A	B	C	CH	D	E	F	G	H	I	J	K	L	LL	M	N
31	32	33	34	35	36	37	38	39	40	41	42	43	44	45	46

N	O	P	Q	R	S	T	U	V	W	X	Y	Z
47	48	49	50	51	52	53	54	55	56	57	58	59

24 · A Plan of Operations

You can't expect pears from an elm.

Payday is a happy day in the barracks. The paymaster smiles as he places his precious burden on the table, the paying officer smiles behind the rosters, and the units form happily without anybody shouting orders at them. There is much noise and crowding in the assembly tent.

Well, in the backlands, Conrado also had paydays for his gang. Every two weeks, from the money extorted from the *finca* owners, the chief paid us approximately two hundred pesos each, putting aside a small amount for the expenses of the gang, and keeping the rest for himself. Where did he hide the money he kept? I was never able to find out, but I estimate that in those days he accumulated at least two hundred thousand pesos. The story was that Conrado had a herd of rustled cattle and horses on some grazing land near Vellocino, and that a man named Saúl was in charge of handling the stock.

To return to payday, the *bandoleros* also smile when the money rewards their dishonest efforts. Then *ruanas* are spread under the trees and for several hours they roll the dice (popularly known as Santa Apolonia's teeth). Snake eyes! Six and a fiver! A pair of fours! Bills change hands while the players murmur nervously and the losers spit out their coarse interjections. Others play *fierrito* with Spanish cards, just as in the most respectable and proper *salón* in town.

Conrado took no part in these recreations; he had other tastes. When some thirteen-year-old girl caught his eye, he sent a patrol for her just like that, giving them orders to machete her if she resisted, and to machete her parents if they tried to interfere. The aggrieved parents handed over their daughters to avoid being killed. Country virgins deflowered prematurely by a pervert, the daughters hiding their tears, their grief, and the rage they endured in the rude camp bunk, so that their parents might stay alive.

To gratify the lubricious appetites of the wretched gang, a certain *mayordomo* would bring in women. In the nearby towns, each *bandolero* had his mistress or his sweetheart; the *mayordomo* collected the women in a jeep and then brought them on horseback to the cave or the *cafetal*, which was converted into a veritable brothel.

On one occasion, after the troops had killed several *bandoleros* from Chispas' gang,† the latter came to see Conrado to propose that the two join forces in order to keep operating. At first Conrado said yes, but when Teófilo Rojas (Chispas) indicated that he would assume command, Conrado responded:

"Me taking orders from someone else again? That's not for me. I had enough of that as a soldier in Mosco's gang."

They fell out, insulted one another, and were about to draw weapons.

All this a *bandolero* told me when the two of us were doing sentinel duty while our companions were throwing dice and playing cards.

Zarpazo decided to operate with the gang divided into three squads: Tista would take seven men; Corporal Ochoa, four; and Conrado would keep three. I had the singular privilege of being one of those with Conrado. Tista would control the regions of Villa Rodas and San Isidro; Ochoa was to operate around Modín and las Coloradas; Conrado would be in the vicinity of Morro Azul.

We all received instructions on operating procedures: particular care in using roads, particular care of weapons, particular care not to leave a trail. Before making an attack put on military uniform—*habano* pants, a green shirt, brown combat boots. The rest of the time weak khaki poplin shirt and pants, sombrero, and *ruana*. Uniforms to be hidden in out of the way caves. Before attacking a hacienda, meet with the other groups. Meeting of the group leaders every three

---

†Chispas was the *bandolero* credited with the greatest number of murders.

days; daily communication between groups by means of messenger. When there were troops around and no possibility of ambushing them, stay in hiding. Notice of the day, hour, and place of an action will be given in good time. This was our detailed operating procedure.

Many were the times that I, through some trick or pretext, managed to get down to the house of the informant, who Conrado thought was my uncle, to alert him to an attack. My "uncle" craftily would in some indirect fashion warn the neighbors or secretly inform the troops.

One afternoon I said to Conrado: "There must be a Judas in the gang, because whenever we get ready to make an attack on a place we find the soldiers there. We have to find the stoolie and cut out his tongue!"

This only increased my reliability in Zarpazo's eyes and removed from me any suspicion of treachery.

25 · Blood Bath

Save us, Oh Lord of the universe! —Ecclesiastes

Two or three days before the massacre, the camp bustled with activity. The *bandolero* chief, knowing the region, had selected his victims from among those who lived in the settlement. His lieutenants, who already had the topography of the place etched on their minds, were ordered to draw up an operations map showing the houses to be entered and listing those to be killed and who would kill them, those who would loot the houses, and those who would remain outside as guards. To be on the safe side, before carrying out such a "dangerous" operation, the commander determined with absolute certainty that the troops and the police would be far away.

With what attention those fiends received their sinister assignments! How receptive their diabolical minds were to the most insignificant details!

Along the zigzag trails went the messengers at a short trot toward some distant hacienda to order the preparation of a meal for twelve or fifteen on such and such a day, because at such a place, impossible for the forces of law and order to locate, the band would reassemble after the massacre. It would be very fitting to reward those hellish workers with a sumptuous repast after the blood-letting.

The distant hills stood out in silhouette against God's sun, which was beginning to scatter light over the land, its life-giving rays inviting an honest day's work. This was the scene as Conrado's gang, dressed as *carabineros*, reached the cluster of houses.

Everything was propitious for peace and work. From the poorest huts and the decent houses alike there arose columns of smoke like tokens of happiness. A mother, a wife, or perhaps a daughter, put wood on the fire while the men optimistically prepared to begin the day's struggle.

As the flames made the wood pop and the brands gave off sparks, in the family circle they talked about the next market day, about the money that would have to be paid to the Farmers' Bank, about the summer heat that beat down on the fields, about the price of coffee, about the baptism of the baby who would carry his father's name.

The dog, man's companion since time immemorial, also took part in that early morning euphoria, waiting for a scrap, a warm bone, or a loving word.

Suddenly the *bandoleros* appeared!

"We are *carabineros* . . . government troops. We are here to search the houses in the interest of law and order."

"If you are from the authorities, we'll cooperate," answered the people. The *bandoleros* separated the men from the women and tied the men's hands behind their backs.

Since the executioners knew before hand whom they were to eliminate, they took these victims from the patios and shoved them out to a chosen nearby spot and riddled them with bullets. After the important men of the settlement had been shot, their heads were cut off with a machete.

Workers' blood, the good blood of our rural countrymen,

moistened the dark earth of the *cafetales*. The spray of bullets and the machetes sowed death where before honest hands had sown wealth for the country.

The tears of horrified women and inconsolable children fell to mingle with the spilled blood, while terrified cries and shouts were lost in the hollowness of space or died out over the pure water of the spring.

Machetes, tinted purple, were wiped clean with outrageous brazenness on the grass still wet with the morning dew.

Those animals took everything they could find in the houses: flashlights, axes, shotguns, shoes and clothing kept for Sunday, cigarettes, a few pesos that represented the labor of many months, the Coltejer quilt that covered the hardness of a miserable bed, an alarm clock, even women's underclothing.

Not all the male victims died in that perfidious attack, Certain ones were only wounded, as specified in the operations plan, so that, terrorized by the events, they would depart the region and, seeing themselves alive, they would bless Conrado's clemency, and would think it wise to collaborate with the *bandoleros*. Let three or four live so they can take the news to the authorities; the soldiers will be at least ten hours arriving. Actually, it wasn't necessary for anyone to go to the authorities with the news; the carrion birds, attracted by the smell of death, wheeled about in the sky, signaling by their fateful circling the location of the carnage, now being licked at by the dogs.

The criminals were sated by the massacre, enriched by the spoils from their victims, satisfied at having eliminated several political enemies. They were not at all remorseful about the grief of the abused women, the desolation of the orphans, or the cries of the wounded as they moved by forced march to the assembly point. There they satisfied their appetites and thirst with food and drink brought from the haciendas at the direction of obliging *mayordomos*, and they relaxed by talking of the shooting, the terror of the prisoners, the spectacle of the mutilated bodies.

Thinking back on things, Conrado Salazar told me one day how they once destroyed a settlement when he belonged to Mosco's gang.

"We made an attack," he told me, "on the hacienda El Diamante, part of the municipality of Victoria, in Valle del Cauca. We killed eighteen men and eight women. The boys . . . we cut off their penises and stuck them in their mouths like cigars. Kids under six Mosco tossed into the air and let them land on his knife. After raping the women, the gang cut off their heads. They tied one woman to a post, naked, and cut off her breasts."

And what happened to traitors, Judases who went to the authorities?

It was too bad for a *bandolero* caught in a betrayal. They would tie him to a tree and prick him in the abdomen or on an arm or a leg so that the pain would make him stick out his tongue; then with a razor blade they would cut out that fleshy member, which serves for tasting, for swallowing—and for speaking. When they were satisfied with what they considered sufficient torture and "punishment," they would cut off his head with a machete.

However, the eye of God was above, and He remembered His people.

26 · Of the Drowned Man, Only the Revolver

Time does not have a forelock.

I was going on "official business" to the place where Corporal Ochoa had his command post when I came upon one of Ochoa's men peacefully fishing with hook and line in the Vieja River. He had caught some fish large enough to enter in a fishing tournament, and he was enjoying the delights of a summer day.

"You going to see Corporal Ochoa," the fisherman asked.

"Yes," I replied. "I've got some orders from Conrado."

"Fine, Zarquito. Wait a minute while I take a bath and the two of us can go together."

He took off his clothes and calmly seated himself on a rock at the edge ready to jump into the water. For a moment he sat there naked, looking at the strong current, not daring to dive in.

All the while I was thinking about the number of deaths carried by those bare shoulders, deaths with which he was not even charged and for which he would never be tried. He was a ghoul who could cut off someone's head with the same equanimity with which he pulled a fish from the water.

He was a real veteran of the gang organized by Zarpazo, and at any moment that hand playing in the water could fire the shot that would kill me or toss the grenade that would mutilate innocent soldiers or unfortunate civilians.

One makes one's own opportunities. We were in a revolutionary war, so I made up my mind and, going over to the rock, I hit the *bandolero* in the head with the butt of my carbine, knocking him senseless into the turbulent river. Then I threw in his clothes and hid his revolver.

The old saying properly goes "of the drowned man, the hat," meaning the hat is the only trace. In this case I could say "of the drowned man, the revolver."

Some hours later when Conrado's people gathered in Buenos Aires to plan a new attack, Corporal Ochoa reported that one of his men had "flown."

Zarpazo, alarmed by the news and fearing the deserter might have gone to the police, ordered our immediate departure from the vicinity.

"Zarquito, will you take my watch?"

"Sure, what time are you on?"

From one to three A.M."

Without Conrado's knowing it, I often took guard duty

for those who were particularly lazy or tired. Thus I gained the confidence of the *bandoleros* and I could also talk with other guards without suspicion.

Watching the stars twinkling that night, I imagined I could hear the swirling of the Vieja River, in whose disturbed waters a *bandolero* had found his grave. My fellow guard brought me out of these thoughts.

"Zarco, this Zarpazo is a mean one. There's no fooling around with him."

"Oh? What do you mean?" I asked.

"He's somebody to be afraid of. He has no respect for God . . . or the devil."

He wanted to share some confidence with me but did not dare.

"Spit it out, buddy," I said. "I've got a few things to talk about, too."

"Well, get this, Zarco. A few months ago the guerrilla action was over on the other side of the mountains. The troops had followed us and Conrado was scared. This kid, maybe twelve years old, barefooted, dressed in rags, came up to our camp; he was out killing birds with a slingshot. Well, Conrado got it into his head that this boy was a spy and he ordered us to kill him on the spot. You just don't disobey Conrado, so with a machete slash we cut off the boy's head. It was easy. It was tender meat!"

To respond to the guard's story, I told one of my own.

In Corporal Trueno's gang, operating around the Magdalena River, there was a kid who hadn't started to be a man yet, called Piojo. When there was killing done the *bandoleros* killed the grown people and let Piojo kill the children. That kid was really a terror at using the machete!*

"Think what he'll be when he grows up," said the guard. "Here comes our relief. Let's get some sleep."

---

*In 1953, around Carare, the *bandolero* Trueno had in his gang a minor, called Piojo, to whom he assigned the killing of children.

27 · The Café Granadino

Pray to God and lay on with the mallet.

Among the curious things that came out of the political violence that lashed our country around 1960 was the partisan political atmosphere found in specific meeting places in certain cities of Valle and Caldas.

In the impassioned city of Cartago, for example, in 1962, the Café Granadino was the favorite collecting place of the Conservatives, while the Liberals frequented the Café La Bolsa.

In the cafés, men find many things: an appropriate place to pass their idle hours; the opportunity to transact business; cards and dice for gaming; liquor to ease one's troubles—or to make one go looking for trouble. In the cafés men eat, they drink, they talk about politics, they "straighten out" the government, they reminisce, they pinch the waitresses, they read the papers, and they fight and . . . they kill!

Through some association of ideas, Conrado, smoldering over the loss of four men to (so be believed) the army, thought about Cartago, and he asked for volunteers to go there and throw two grenades into the Café Granadino. I took a step forward but Zarpazo objected that he did not want me to be killed, for the mission was a dangerous one.

The fact was that I had gained all the confidence that a subaltern can receive from his chief, to the point that Conrado did or did not do just about anything I suggested to him.

Finally he acceded to my request and authorized me to select a companion in the undertaking.

Among the nineteen that remained of the original group was Gata, Tista Tabares' second in command when the gang was divided.

Tista had said to me: "Zarco, you've got to be my second, but you have to kill Gata first. That's for sure. But don't do it in front of me or in front of the other guys, because I have to show that I'm the commander and I'd have to order you killed."

Personal rivalry is a part of daily existence among the *bandoleros*. Tista Tabares hated Gata because this latter animal abused women terribly, and besides that he was a thief raised to the second power. Despite everything, in even the most perverse heart there dwells an infinitesimal particle of morality.

But Gata was far from enthusiastic about the projected grenade-toss. He was suspicious and distrustful, and he was both jealous and afraid of me.

Since Mono had volunteered to go in place of Gata, the former and I went to carry out the mission, armed with "pineapples," revolvers, and pistols.

"You think you can throw a grenade?," I asked him on the way. "Because if you don't think you can, give it to me and I'll throw both of them while you cover my getaway with your pistol."

Dressed in lightweight *ruanas*, we reached the Café Granadino.

In Colombia the *ruana* has all sorts of uses, good and bad. The *bandoleros* and thugs wear it to cover arms and ammunition, thus foiling the vigilance of the detectives, the police, and the soldiers.

That Saturday, at two in the afternoon, the Café Granadino was abustle. Waitresses were bringing brandies, *empanadas*, and beer, and replying to the frequent flirtatious remarks with a smile or a quip, as they generously distributed little cups of fragrant black coffee.

The place was a beehive, a combination of noise, voices, music, shouts, all wrapped in clouds of smoke from Pielroja cigarettes and local cigars.

We stopped near one of the doorways. My companion was frightened almost to death, and he said to me: "Look at those two suspicious looking fellows over there who are watching us."

He was talking about two simple vendors standing behind their carts at the corner.

"Yeah," I replied. "Those are dangerous guys."

"Don't throw the grenades," he begged, "because those two detectives will get us."

"What the hell! . . . that's what *you're* here for . . . to back me up and to cream them if that's necessary," I answered.

Then getting a little closer to the door and pointing out four men who were playing billiards, I whispered to him. "Mono, those are police," I lied. "There's no problem with them. When I toss the grenade, they die right there inside."

Looking toward the corner, I continued: "Those fellows over there are fuzz, too, in street clothes. I'm going to throw one grenade through this door and the second through the other door. And then look out, brother, because we're really going to start shooting!"

My companion's fear was now beyond all bounds, and this was exactly what I was working for. I had to appear to Mono to be completely heartless and utterly fearless.

"I'm going over to the john," I whispered. "You stay here by the door. When I come running out I'll throw a grenade and I'll cover my retreat with the other one. You start shooting, but be careful not to hit me!"

I went over to the washroom. When I came out Mono had fled and was already past the office of the Expreso Palmira.

Before returning to Conrado's camp I gave an account of the incident to the chief of the DAS in Cartago and warned him to be alert since Zarpazo would insist on having the grenades thrown. I asked them to be watchful, and having delayed only long enough to give the information, I again took the road back to the woods.

At Coloradas the following exchange took place:

MONO: "I thought they had killed you . . ."

ZARCO: "How the devil could they kill me if there was no-
            body there! But you, you crud, you took off and
            left me there alone. And what you told Conrado
            about the café being full of police and detectives
            is a black lie."

CONRADO: "Then, Zarco, why didn't you throw the

grenades?"

ZARCO: "What's the point in throwing grenades and getting yourself killed, too? The smart thing is to be able to throw them and then come back and tell you about it and get paid for it. I'm sure not going to throw them free for nothing.

"Say, Mono's running out on me is a real serious thing in this business. Those sorry devils that don't do what they are supposed to do will get somebody else killed."

The scene was successfully played. As the curtain fell, Conrado Salazar—judge, prosecutor, and jury of the gang—condemned the wretched Mono to death.

One shot more, one *bandolero* less.

28 · Sentry Dogs

Beware the dog.

The comings and goings to those out of the way places, leaving one place to camp in another, made it possible for me to learn all the band's hideouts.

My mission was progressing well, but to complete it, it would be necessary to get rid of the leaders—which I could not do without getting killed myself. The information I possessed would facilitate the 8th Brigade's wiping out several gangs. Therefore, before finishing off Conrado, Tista, and Ochoa, I had to have a plan for escape.

At a meeting, Tista Tabares asked Conrado for permission to take me in his patrol. Although Zarpazo was somewhat uneasy because of the casualties and the desertions, and although he wanted me with him, he gave Tista permission.

Those were three solid weeks of misery and hardship, all because Tista was very cautious. He wouldn't allow us to sleep in houses but only out in the *cafetales* and on the most rugged and inaccessible slopes. We had to sleep with our legs straddling a coffee tree and our feet tied together on the other side so that we wouldn't roll down the steep slope in our sleep.

He said the troops never searched the passes, just in the settlements, on level stretches, and in the gullies. He traveled with two dogs. The police and the army used sheep dogs in their work, and Tista also had two barking dogs, which he would tether at certain spots to announce the presence of soldiers by their barking. The soldiers would attach no importance to finding a dog tied to a tree and yet the animals were our real lookouts, on duty day and night. On three occasions, I witnessed their effectiveness.

But one fine day they were found poisoned and no one could imagine who would conceive or carry out the "canicide."

I felt the *bandoleros* were about to get wise to me, but the one who was about to denounce me was a *mayordomo*, an assiduous collaborator with Conrado and his men. The only thing I could do was to force the issue. It was the *mayordomo* or me!

By devious means I managed to obtain some cyanide and, suddenly confronting Tista and feigning indignation, I said:

"Now I know who poisoned the dogs. Look, I found this at the *mayordomo's* house."

Tista refused to believe me because the *mayordomo* had performed many services for him. So later in a meeting with Conrado's patrol, I again pulled out my red herring.

"I found out who the traitor is! I've got the proof."

I repeated my accusations, exaggerating them to the utmost. That afternoon the collaborator was no longer. They gave Corporal Ochoa the job of "removing" the fellow.

That same day Gata asked Tista for permission to go to Montenegro. He did not return.

29 · Mutiny Aboard

Divide and conquer.

The chief ordered Escalera and another man to go to a certain place to pick up five thousand pesos that had been promised him.

"When those guys get back I'm going to give you a thousand," Conrado said to me. "And then you're going to Tuluá to bring back ammunition."

We waited a day and a night. At dawn the following day, Escalera not having returned, the gang moved to El Chuzo.

When one of the *bandoleros* takes longer than expected to carry out a mission, it is assumed that there has been a betrayal, and it is necessary to change location in order to avoid being surprised. This is the reason the troops frequently fail to find the *bandoleros*, even though the information supplied was quite accurate. Conrado knew very well that the several authorities in Valle and Caldas had put a price on his head and would pay good money for an opportune betrayal.

Escalera and his pal showed up some days later, accompanied by a woman, and told Conrado they had spent three thousand pesos in the spree—and if he didn't like it, let him do something about it!

"What do you think, Tiro?" Zarpazo asked me. I have forgotten to note that besides "Zarco" they had given me other nicknames. "What do you think about what these lousy so-and-so's have done?"

"The money they spent isn't all that much," I replied. "The serious thing is bringing that woman here. She'll know our hideout and later she may rat on us."

Enraged by the insubordination of his men and the unauthorized waste of the money, Conrado shouted: "I'm going to kill these studs!"

"Leave 'em to me," I urged, pretending to be indignant over the conduct of Escalera and his pal.

I called them over and as they approached I berated

them: "You no-good bums! Why did you waste three thousand pesos carousing around? Conrado owed me that money, and you did me out of it."

"Aw, you want to be boss, but you ain't got the muscle," they answered, and they were pulling out their revolvers to drill me. But I, obeying my instantaneous reflexes, emptied my weapon at them, right under Conrado Salazar's nose.

The outburst of protest from our companions was unanimous. They threatened Conrado and they threatened me. They blamed him for letting me do whatever I wanted to do, and they said I was decimating the gang.

The situation was extremely explosive. A sign of weakness or fear would remove me permanently from the scene. So, making a brave front, I raised my voice and declared:

"We have one leader and that's Conrado Salazar and his orders will be carried out regardless. I want you to know and understand that I'll see that they're carried out, even if I get killed doing it; because I do my duty. And if one of you wants me out of the gang, try to get rid of me—if you think you can!"

I said this looking over my shoulder at the mutineers and patting my still-smoking carbine.

The rapidity of the shots that had just finished off the two rebels must have inspired some fear in the others because once the hot words were over their tempers cooled off and they buried the dead men.

Conrado's prestige was saved and the principle of authority was secured. Saved also was my hide. And society was well rid of two very undesirable individuals.

In the following days the heavens suddenly opened up and St. Peter let fall on us all the rain in the sky. Rain fell night and day, at times accompanied by tornadic winds or flashes of lightning that would suddenly light up the area. Then would come tremendous claps of thunder, as if all the pieces of an artillery battalion were firing at the same time; the deafening vibrations seemed to make the *guamos* tremble and the palm trees shudder. Then Conrado, who had a lot of experience in this, divided us into groups and sent us to houses in the vicinity. He felt that the troops would not be coming around while the torrential downpour lasted.

However, the troops had learned that storms or just rain could be their very good allies in surprise attacks against the *bandoleros*; many a successful action was carried out in the driving rain.

But summer or winter the forced contributions continued, causing bitter frustration for those who possessed rich lands and could not enjoy them. This is a torment comparable to that of Tantalus, who was punished by Jupiter and who is represented as standing in the middle of a river "whose waters recede as his lips approach the surface; he is also directly beneath a cluster of fruit hanging from a limb that rises just out of reach when he tries to grasp the fruit."

When will all this end, the disconsolate *hacendados* asked themselves, as they brooded on their bitterness and their frustration.

30 · The Supply Convoy

They went for wool and returned shorn.

The precipitousness of our terrain has made it easy for the *bandoleros* to ambush troops bringing supplies to their comrades in arms. The lack of equipment, the steepness of the terrain, and the bad weather (so frequent in our *cordilleras*) make it impractical to supply the military posts by helicopter.

For the *bandoleros* the ascent of the supply convoy (popularly called *la remesa*) is a temptation, because if they can carry off the attack successfully they are supplied with food, drugs, uniforms, arms, and ammunition.

However, when the troop escort makes proper use of its scouts, the *bandoleros* go out for wool—and are themselves shorn.

"The supply train comes today!" is a phrase that stirs the bodies and spirits of those who serve the flag in distant parts. What hopes, what dreams those words arouse in men who long for a letter from their parents, news about a sweetheart, a newspaper, fresh food to restore their strength, cigarettes and matches, batteries for the transistor radios—or maybe head-quarters is sending new clothing. And the payroll might come, too—those centavos that really are not a salary but rather a loving token from the country to its sacrificing sons. And the barber may come; if not, there will be new scissors.

The eyes of the sentinel study the horizon, anticipating the appearance of the supply convoy, with its trailing cloud of dust as it moves along the highway.

Tired of the life I was leading with Tista, I returned to Zarpazo. I was drained, exhausted, fearful that asleep or awake I might say a word that would betray me. The nervous tension was pushing me to the limit of my endurance and, frankly, my spiritual springs were about to snap.

At the meeting of the leaders Conrado informed Tista that the next Sunday supplies would be coming up the moun-tain to the military post at Villarrodas. Tista, very skilled in these affairs, would ambush the convoy.

Before the impending tragedy could take place, I sought permission to go down to see my "uncle," to get some clothes, I said, but my intention was to alert the informer. But Conrado did not let me go.

Could Zarpazo be getting suspicious?

Careful, careful, Pelusa, I said to myself. ("Pelusa" was another nickname the gang gave me.) Watch it! You know the pitcher that goes to the well too often finally gets broken.

I was overwhelmed, lacking the remotest possibility of help.

Tista and three of his men were down with the Asiatic or Korean flu, but despite their illness the attack on the convoy would still take place on Sunday. Conrado thought about putting Corporal Ochoa in charge of the operation, but Ochoa and his men were in Quimbaya.

"Well, I'm here and I can replace Tista," I remarked to Zarpazo.

The suggestion seemed to strike him as a good one. He immediately approved, and on the spot I became his second in command.

Sunday morning the chief came up to me and said: "It's been confirmed that the supplies are coming up. Take five men."

"Don't worry about it," I responded. "Today we will have new weapons and ammunition, salt, medicine, uniforms, and boots."

"I hope you don't get yourselves killed," observed Conrado.

"I'm sure not going to get myself killed, like that. If those other stoops let themselves get killed, that's something else. If they kill me," I added, "I'll take quite a few of those *chulos* with me."

"I'll stay at Naranjos," said Conrado. "If I hear much shooting, I'll come help you."

Conrado left and I went to ambush the troops.

Seated on the side of a ravine I tried to organize my thoughts, which were a painful, confused jumble in my head—the warmth of the hearth, the love of my wife, my daughters, my mother, and my brothers and sisters; our country, Colombia, so rich, so beautiful, and served by such self-sacrificing sons as the soldiers and the police, who even gave their lives to return peace to its martyred regions. Through my mind passed my comrades in the San Mateo, from the brigade. I seemed to hear the voices of the captain, the lieutenant, the sergeant.

Was now the time to return to my unit? Might my comrades be with the convoy today? The Lord's day was made to be a day of rest, at least in town . . .

"Hey, Pelusa," shouted one of the men, who had more gumption than the others. "Is this where we're going to set up the trap, or what?"

"You men know the region better than I, so you pick the spots. What you decide will be all right," I shouted back. "I'll

take the rear truck and you all take the front one."
They began to talk about the action:
"From here we can wipe them out."
"Near the field, where there's room to run."
"Be sure to get the drivers and the commander."
"No need to leave even one for seed."
My mind was breaking. I must save the soldiers. If I did
something impulsive and fired to alert them, Zarco would be
finished as a *bandolero*.

Suddenly I had a good thought. The five men were carrying on their conversation grouped together. I thought no
more. I took my cut down carbine in my right hand and my
.38 long in my left and I fired!

Far away more shots sounded. Were those from the soldiers or from the *bandoleros*?

"Sergeant, the fingertips of the five dead men have been
mutilated so the fingerprints cannot be identified. Here are
all their guns and ammunition. Fortunately this was so well
hidden the *bandoleros* didn't find it."

"Five San Cristóbal carbines and twenty magazines full of
ammunition. Well done, Buitrago! What do you plan to do
now?"

"Return to my detachment, sergeant, and report to my
colonel that I'm all present and accounted for. I can't go
back to the gang. I consider my mission completed. Conrado's band is practically broken up."

"How did all this happen?"

"The five men were killed instantly in the burst from my
carbine. I took their weapons and cartridge belts and hid it all
beside a rock. Then I went quickly to the place where Conrado was supposed to be, to tell him the soldiers had surprised us. I was going to kill him and those with him. But
Conrado had already left Naranjos. I tried to pick up his trail,
but it was no use. It was seven in the evening by then. I went
back and picked up the weapons and headed down the canyon. I had to rest; I slept until eleven at night. I woke up
with a start. Then I hid the weapons near a ravine and con-

tinued down the mountain, keeping the Madsen rifle hidden under my *ruana*.

"At one in the morning a pair of lovers were having a drink at the *cantina* in Garajes. Outside a truck was parked. I asked the gentleman please to take me to Zarzal or Cartago. His refusal was accompanied by a string of insults. So I pulled my gun and tied up and gagged the fellow, the woman, and the proprietor. Then driving the vehicle myself, I came to Zarzal.

"The rest you know, sergeant. It's a good thing you helped me and that we came right away back to where these things happened. If we had waited a few hours we would not have found the weapons."

31 · Exodus

Your sorrow is as great as the sea.

Down the roads that scar the hillsides file those who have been driven from the settlements, men and women of all sorts and conditions. Each holds something: an article of clothing, perhaps a Fabricato quilt, a dish, a hoe, something saved from *la violencia*.

There they go, quickening the pace as they approach the city, which will open its gates to them. There the inhabitants, rich and poor, will look at them, first with compassion, and then with curiosity and then with indifference, as if they were watching a live, skinned cow being led by its master through the town. They move forward facing the sun and the wind and leave a trail dampened by their tears. They have abandoned their planted fields, the coffee trees heavy with berries, the full uddered cows, the bountiful garden that year after year supplied the family with food in abundance.†

The women, in bright colored dresses, pat the babes that cling to their breasts. The men in their white *ruanas*, some with a bag of possessions tied on their backs, try to light a cigar. Already they can hear the muffled noise of the city; they can see the comings and goings of the pedestrians; now they can hear the strident blarings of horns. Who will give them shelter as they aimlessly wander the asphalt streets? Who will help the strangers, who hardly could know and be known by the owner of the big store, or the merchant who sells on credit guaranteed by the prospect of payday, or the priest who year after year pours the holy water over the babies of his own flock?

And their fellow refuges, can they perhaps pay back the fifty or so pesos owed, when these comrades, also exiled by the *bandoleros*, are only thankful to heaven they were able to escape with their lives?

Tomorrow when they wake up in a miserable room or lying on a floor somewhere with no money to buy things and no place to build a fire, then they will long for their beloved *finca*, with its column of smoke rising to heaven, and the water from the brook that slakes the thirst of man and animal; then they will feel the full weight of their tragedy. Closed in by four walls grudgingly conceded by some pseudo-philanthropic relative, they no longer will look to the good Lord's sun to determine the hour for beginning and ending the day's work. Nor will they study the clouds, or feel the joy of the rain, which is happiness, life, and hope for the countryside.

"Daddy, why do we have to leave the *finca*?" asks a distressed lad, and his unanswered question is carried off by the wind that tosses the branches of the coffee trees.

What a difference between the exodus of today and the

---

†While it is true that thousands of refugees from *la violencia* came to Colombian cities between 1946 and 1965, there was also a general rural-to-urban migration process going on during the same years. Only a fraction of these urban immigrants can be definitely attributed to *la violencia*.

Sunday procession to the little parish church, and the subsequent stroll to the marketplace, past the city hall, the Coffee Federation building, and the Farmers' Bank.

Good country people, the soul of Colombia, with their roots in the land that gave them birth or that generously received them when, tired from their traveling, they seated themselves beside its fountain! With these refugees come their faithful dogs, which stop every instant as if they understood their masters' bewildering grief; for these country dogs there will also be a forced confinement, and when they furtively venture out to the street they will find some morsel filled with strychnine which, after a long agony, will put an end to their life's journey on earth!

I watch the procession, the civilians driven out by the *bandoleros* who, with blood and fire, took possession of their lands! I watch the procession that has shed all its tears and has no other baggage than its bitterness!

32 · Vignettes of *Bandolero* Life

"They woke up here, they ate there; at times they fled, not knowing from whom; other times they waited, not knowing for whom. They slept standing up, interrupting their sleep to move from one place to another. It was ever a matter of spies being sent out, sentinels listening, harquebusiers blowing on their matches . . ."—Cervantes describing the life of the *cuadrilla* of *bandoleros* captained by Roque de Guinart in the vicinity of Barcelona

This chapter is just an account of some aspects of the life of the *cuadrilla* (gang), a life of sudden attacks, of hiding places, of agonizing uncertainty.

The life of the *bandolero* in the bush is like that of the owl, that nocturnal bird of ill omen that begins its day when the shades of night take possession of the earth.

Our *cuadrilla* (I am referring to Conrado's, the one I infiltrated) took advantage of the night when making its marches to new camp sites or scouting an objective. While the sun sent its blessed and healthful light over the earth, we hid ourselves in the *cafetales*, in the shade of huge *guamos* or that of sheltering banana trees.

Breakfast and the noonday meal were brought to us at the appointed time by collaborationists, usually *mayordomos* or administrators from the larger haciendas, as if it were a matter of bringing food to honest workers. In the *cuadrilla* one constantly lives in atmosphere of fear—fear of the troops, of the police, of their own collaborators, and even of their fellow *bandoleros*. If one of the men does not return promptly from a mission assigned, then the alarm is out and everyone is uneasy because the missing man could have surrendered to the authorities, or he may have been captured, or he might simply have turned traitor in order to collect a considerable reward.

Who can be sure of the word or of the integrity of a *bandolero*? As the old saying goes, "A thief who steals from a thief gets a hundred days' pardon."

For this reason, when there was a new man in the band the first thing Conrado ordered was that he be photographed fully armed. On the next attack this photo would be left on the body of some victim so that the new recruit would be irrevocably implicated, so far as the authorities were concerned, and would be afraid to be seen publicly.

There are many security measures, and upon them depends the life of the *cuadrilla*. As an instance, no one in our band could have his clothes washed at any place except the one designated by Conrado.

As can be seen in some chapters of this account, the men obtained permission from the chiefs in order to go into town and have their fun. On such occasions they would go in pairs and at a time when the authorities were not checking too closely on people in town.

When they wanted to satisfy their thirst for alcohol, without leaving the *cafetales* and with the appropriate security guards, they concentrated on drinking; they saturated themselves with liquor they sent for or that was given to them. These sylvan carousals would end up in a wenching spree with camp followers, some of them volunteers, others girls who had been carried off by force.

On the subject of women, whenever the gang carried out an attack, the young girls captured were distributed among the members of the band. Some *bandoleros*, not satisfied with raping them, made them follow the band by threatening them, if they resisted, with the death of the father or a brother. Once in the hideout, the poor girl accepted a new master when the first one had to be away on a mission.

We were never without information about what was happening in other parts of the country because we had two or three transistor radios, and also because obliging people in Cartago and Montenegro saw to it that the man who collected milk brought us copies of *El Tiempo, El Espectador, El País,* and the local papers of Armenia and Cartago.

It was impossible to communicate with one's family. Letter writing was absolutely forbidden; letters might betray us. Only when someone happened along who was of proved reliability were we permitted to send a few pesos home.

To heal wounds and treat the diseases that abounded in the backlands, we had a Chinese ointment, said to have been brought from Buenaventura, that gave relief from toothache and headache. However, there was no shortage of self-appointed doctors for diagnoses and treatments of questionable value. As the saying goes, "Everybody has a touch of the doctor, the poet, and the madman."

A sort of medical technician-aid man, or an apprentice, always accompanied the band, performing simple procedures and giving us shots, the latter so inexpertly done that a cyst almost always resulted.

But there was no need for doctors or even medics, what with a "prayer" that Conrado Salazar confided to a few of his most intimate associates. It was a strange prayer indeed, calling on the Almighty to keep away evil while one was forgetting God and killing one's neighbor without compassion. This mixture of Christianity and witchcraft, a brew from the Middle Ages, revealed a crass ignorance of religious matters.

But Conrado and his confidants had absolute faith in this mechanical invocation, and to it they attributed their success in raids or in combat with the government forces. Here is the "prayer," which makes one invisible, and which must be said with faith and kept in absolute secrecy so as to be effective:

> With three I see you,
> With five I bind you.
> Your blood I let stream
> And your heart I split.
> Christ, behold me
> And deliver me from all evil.
> Here comes my enemy.
> Oh, just Judge:
> if he has eyes,
> may he not see me;
> if he has hands,
> may they not touch me;
> if he has weapons,
> may they not harm me.
> Santa Cruz de Mayo,
> go to my house;
> deliver me from harm
> and from Satan.
>   AMEN

A gasoline lantern, of the gas-mantle type, shining at odd hours of the night, indicated a *bandolero* encampment. Such lights were part of a code of signals used by the *bandoleros* and their collaborators to announce a clear path, the presence of troops, the departure of the police, danger, etc.

A flashlight or hand lantern was everyone's inseparable companion; so all who are on a mission must not fail to notice a set of discarded batteries or a burned out bulb or the intermittent flashing of lights—the *bandoleros* are nearby!

What about the supplying of ammunition? I can testify that the munitions that reached Conrado's *cuadrilla* came from the cities and were supplied by persons who were considered respectable—people of some political importance. (Further information relating to this is in the possession of my superiors.)

When we were prepared for an undertaking of some size, with the uniforms and the weapons we had the appearance of real *carabineros*. Military uniforms were very scarce because the *bandoleros* came into possession of one only when some soldier deserted and came to the mountains. Such a desertion is a sad exception, but it paradoxically only serves to prove the rule of loyalty and unity in the military forces.†

Before the departure of night patrols or especially important missions, Conrado would pass out to the men dried marijuana leaves, which, wrapped in cigarette paper and smoked, would produce a state of mind expansion, as if the mind were separated from the body. While this intoxication lasted the men felt no fear or weariness or scruples. Thus one more criminal act was added to the interminable series of crimes! But Conrado did not smoke the abominable weed because he knew the consequences, knew the toxic effect, knew that it separated body and spirit. I pretended to smoke those cigarettes, but I threw them away at the first opportunity.

When marijuana was not available Conrado distributed little pieces of *mejoral*, a stimulant that was cut into tiny bits and mixed with cobwebs. This was smoked eagerly by the men, and it produced an even greater state of disorientation than marijuana did.

The spirit of Satan illuminated Zarpazo's perverse mind and took control of those alienated, misguided Colombians.

---

†Buitrago's pride in the infrequency of Colombian military desertions after 1953 is completely justified. However, he was evidently unaware that bogus military and police uniforms abound in many rural areas, thanks to illicit uniform manufacturers who smuggled them, like the weapons and ammunition, from urban sources to rural *bandolero* units.

33 · Conrado Tries to Get Pelusa

He who hits first, hits twice.

I was on an interesting assignment near the railroad station in Cartago. Because of my appearance, my dress, and the vehicle I was driving I could easily pass for a hacienda owner or a worker from those parts.

To be able to smell danger must be one of the attributes of the soldier, one that he acquires through experience and training. Therefore, after leaning against the truck for half an hour, I turned my head to look at a man who was approaching.

It was Trasnocho, a former comrade in Zarpazo's gang. He stood looking at me intently and I returned his stare. Out of the corner of my eye I could see two others following him, none other than Zancudo and Mariposo, both also agents for Zarpazo and Company.

I wanted to get into the truck and drive away, but to try to do so would be suicide. In one jump I was behind the truck with my revolver drawn. I didn't give them time to open fire; the three criminals fell, gunned down with their pistols in hand. What wisdom is contained in the old saying, "He who hits first, hits twice!"

Conrado Salazar had failed in his first attempt to eliminate me.

I grabbed the *bandoleros'* guns and left the scene before the police arrived. At the hotel I changed clothes and put on sunglasses; then I sauntered down to the station to join the crowd of curious onlookers surrounding the bodies.

The DAS men dashed around very excitedly because in the "Who's Who Among the Criminals" the dead men had entire chapters describing their crimes.

The *vita* of Trasnocho can be synthesized in a few sentences: he was a hardened *bandolero*. Taken prisoner in Cartago and sent to Zarzal, he promised to lead the authorities to a certain spot, reportedly to turn over weapons; although handcuffed, he managed to escape, leaving no trail. Zancudo had belonged to Chispas' *cuadrilla*. His joining Conrado Salazar came about this way, according to an account he had given me months before: One day Teófilo Rojas Varón, alias Chispas, sent an eight-man patrol to bushwhack a few *carabineros* near La Polonia, above Carniceros, almost at the border of La Línea. The supposed *carabineros* turned out to be the gang of Efraín González, and they, being more alert, got the drop on Chispas' men and killed five of them. Zancudo, terrified by the event, went to seek refuge in Conrado's *cuadrilla*.

Efraín González, a native of Pijao, Caldas, wanted to kill Chispas because the latter had ordered the murder of a relative of Efraín. That was a time when the *lex taxionis* raised to the second power held sway within the *bandolero* family.

Efraín González was continually challenging Chispas, but the latter was afraid of him. Don Efraín was not exactly a dove. And to think that a fellow Colombian has demanded a court martial for a distinguished army colonel, the one responsible for the death of this *bandolero*, who brought misery and mourning to the peaceful regions of Santander and Boyacá. . . . †

Mariposo, a subaltern of Cenizas, escaped death by throwing himself to the floor when the troops of the Codazzi battalion surprised him at a dance. When the shooting stopped Mariposo seized an instrument and passed himself off as one of the musicians. He was detained but released for lack of evidence after three weeks. The menace this man represented surpasses imaginable limits. Following his detention, he killed the girl he was courting and her father because she

---

†Chispas survived several inter-*cuadrilla* battles before his final demise at the hands of an army-engineer battalion in 1963. Efraín González, with a lower record of murders than Chispas, came originally from Santander, not Caldas. He was killed by the army in a celebrated Bogotá gun battle in June, 1965. Even though five soldiers were killed in trying to capture González alive, the army was still irresponsibly criticized for having killed him, and Buitrago's bitterness shows here.

did not wish to accompany him. To avoid the consequences of this terrible crime, he fled to a sugar mill at Pradera, where he forced the owner and his wife to give him food and shelter.

Discovered by Elefantico, from Conrado's *cuadrilla*, and invited to do so, Mariposo joined Zarpazo's ranks.

34 · A Traveling Salesman

He who has enemies does not sleep.

A traveling salesman is a respectable citizen, the representative of one or more business firms. As the name indicates, he travels over God's earth to the towns, cities, and villages of the district, selling his merchandise, "quality but inexpensive," and earning a good commission in the process. This is a pleasant occupation, enjoyable and lucrative, and in it the man who talks best sells most.

There are many types of traveling salesmen, and all that stuff about "equality" that the demagogues cackle about does not exist in heaven, or on earth, or in the depths of hell.

I was using the cover of a traveling salesman, the type called a *cascarero*, a purveyor of rather shoddy goods—nylon socks for men (three pairs for five pesos), and of a face powder that contained mostly flour.

However undynamic I tried to be and despite the fact that I put a high price on these wares so the merchants would not order from me, honest citizens did sometimes bite. One such person was a storekeeper in Zarzal; he wanted to order quite a number of things, and so I was obliged to go to Manizales to fetch merchandise so as to maintain my front. Thus through performance and function I became a real traveling salesman, with leather satchel, papers, invoices, and sunglasses.

I was staying at the Hotel Sevillana in Cartago and I was

flirting with one of the maids, because such carrying on is considered a part of this work. The girl was, as the hip teenagers say, "hooked on me," because in addition to the pleasantries, the banter, and the promises I was always making to her, from my traveling salesman satchel came pairs of stockings and pieces of material that I presented to her with great gallantry.

This was a third-rate hotel with enormous rooms that were divided by wooden partitions into small rooms, each furnished with an iron cot, a straw mattress and pillow, and cheap muslin sheets.

There was a common bath; that is to say, it conformed to the old motto "one for all and all for one"; it had very little toilet paper and very little ventilation. They used to say in the hotel that there were no fleas because the bedbugs ate them and, in truth, a number of the latter sustained themselves on the guests' blood.

Through that flophouse, that democratic condominium, passed an endless procession of people from the country and from neighboring towns. These transient boarders were alien to the refinements that civilization has brought, and their poverty or their underdevelopment made them tolerant of even the most flagrant offenses against good hygiene.

One Saturday, about ten in the evening, Teresa came to my room and in a low voice said:

"Don Jaime, in number twelve there are two fellows who have belts with cartridges stuck in them and they're carrying some things that look like grenades. They sent me for a bottle of liquor. They're bad men; let's tell the police."

"Buy them the liquor; take them two bottles, and then try to get the police."

The night was hot and the mosquitos, in successive waves, made their annoying, bloodsucking attack against ankles, ears, throats, and hands.

From my satchel I took a rope and tied it to a big meat hook. Using this as a grappling hook, I tossed it to the beam below the ceiling; it caught and held. In three pulls I climbed to the top of the partition and could look down into the other room. I saw two men from Tista Tabares' gang, saturated with alcohol. On the night table were two MK-2 grenades, two revolvers, some knives, and a cartridge belt.

To wait until the police arrived was to give the *bandoleros* an opportunity to kill two or three of the self-sacrificing officers; and then, too, these two might even escape. So without thinking about it further I moved the hook to the other side, slid down the rope, and landed on top of them.

The death struggle was brief, hand to hand, no guns.

The traveling salesman, after eliminating two of the worst criminals and being wounded, but not seriously, disappeared from the hotel. A few minutes later the DAS men arrived.

I learned some time later that the government of Valle del Cauca had paid twenty thousand pesos reward for the information given the authorities by the maid, and that she had taken her mother to live in Tolima.

35 · The Wall

Valor is better than numbers and ability is superior to valor.

El Paredon! The wall! The firing squad! Execution! When we hear those words our flesh creeps at the recollection of the acts of the bearded tyrant of the Caribbean.†

Many compatriots speak of the wall, the firing squad, as if it were a panacea for the ills of our country. There is some justification for it if it is used to punish atrocities or treason, whether the treason benefits internal elements or foreign

---

†When Buitrago was writing this book, Premier Fidel Castro was attempting to implant or infiltrate three rural armed gangs in the Colombian backlands. While Buitrago recognized the difference between criminals and revolutionaries, he also knew that the Colombian soldier could expect death at the hands of either.

powers. Bolívar said: "Clemency to criminals is an attack on virtue."

In times of the Conquest the Spanish resolved their problems with a rope and a tree. At least in Peru, according to the author Ricardo Palma, hanging was used with discretion, possibly to save ammunition. Since we have been talking about the wall, let us return to Quimbaya and attend the Sunday matinee. They were showing a cowboy movie.

About four in the afternoon as I was leaving the show, I was seized by three men dressed as policemen.

"So you finally got caught," they said to me.

They hit me at their pleasure. I knew immediately these were "legitimate" *bandoleros* and I truly was afraid. I forgot to say that they searched me and took my revolver. Then they literally kicked me into a car.

"Where are you taking me?"

"The Inspector of Police at Paraíso wants to see you. We're going there."

"Why, I've never even been there."

"Well, he wants to see you and that's that."

A couple of miles from Quimbaya we left the highway and followed a dirt road for a short distance; then we stopped.

"Get out!" they ordered.

"There's no police station here," I said.

"Get out, you S.O.B.!" they shouted.

Shoving and pushing they stood me with my hands behind me and my back to an embankment. I was at the wall; I faced the firing squad.

"So this is the dandy gunslinger of the Quindío! Why don't you try that with us? You always kill people when there's no risk to you!"

"Any time I ever killed anybody I was risking my life. I killed them fighting and I kill men who have weapons in their hands to defend themselves. I don't kill defenseless people, the way you do."

With my words I hoped to divert the *bandoleros* or at least gain a little time until I saw some chance to save myself.

One of the trio pushed me and hit me in the face. Another said to him:

"Let him talk. Let him say what he wants, because he's going to die anyhow."

I kept on talking, asking them to give me a chance, to let me run, whenever they said, and then they could shoot at me.

"Your only chance, you traitorous toad, is that you can count to ten; maybe at ten we'll change our minds." They laughed.

They were playing with me as the cat does with the mouse he catches. They asked me about myself, as if they were judges. I told them I was an orphan, a single fellow, traveling around, and for that reason I had taken up the adventurous life. I assured them, further, that the government of Tolima was offering sixty thousand pesos reward for me, dead or alive; and I said if they collected the money, I hoped they would remember me.

"The talking's over. Start counting!"

There was no way out. When I reached "ten" I would be out of this world and into the next.

Four revolvers were pointed at me, three from the *bandolero* arsenal plus the one they had taken from me, which one of the *bandoleros* was waving around in his left hand.

"You're counting too slow."

Just as I finished "seven" I slipped out the forty-five I carried hidden in my belt at my back and, quick as lightning, and with the precision of a champion marksman, I shot all three.† Two fell dead and the third, mortally wounded and agonized with pain, after a few seconds managed to gasp:

"Now I believe what they say . . . that you're 'helped' . . .

---

†North American readers will notice the obvious possibility that Buitrago's memory of this incident may have been colored by his great interest in Hollywood westerns. However, no one should question the author's bravery and skill with weapons, even if this incident appears to have been somewhat embellished in the telling.

that you have a pact with the devil . . . because all of a sudden you have a gun in your hand."

"No pacts with the devil. It's just you didn't frisk me properly, and then you let yourselves get fooled by my talk. Luck and a quick draw, that's all."

He died shortly afterward. He was the one who had hit me, the one who told me to count faster so they could kill me sooner.

Valor is better than numbers, and ability is superior to valor.

The next day the papers carried stories of the recovery of a car stolen in Salento and the finding of three dead *bandoleros*, for whom the government of Valle had offered a reward.

36 · Hand Grenades

No one dies before his time.

I was sent again to the San Mateo Battalion—for a rest. In truth, my work with the Mobile Intelligence Group had been exhausting.

For a month, I was commander of the Military Police. The soldiers liked me because I treated them well. Modesty aside, I had something of the gift of command, that ability to make oneself be obeyed and to exercise influence over subordinates, as the military manual teaches us.

But after a month I was assigned to the training battery, and that was not my specialty. Bored with these professional duties, so necessary but as monotonous as close-order drill, I requested (from Major L.L. and Colonel V.V., both of the 8th Brigade) a return to intelligence work. This time they gave me four noncoms, selected from all those who comprised the Operations Unit.

Once more in my element, practicing my military specialty, as Personnel would say, I resumed my activities.

In B-2, the Intelligence Section, they received information that Conrado Salazar was in the vicinity of Buenos Aires. With two informants, I went to verify this report. After three days of tiresome waiting our field rations ran out, so I left the informants at a lookout spot and went down to a house to buy some sugar cake. Thus this *panela—chancaca* they call it in Peru—was to give me lead poisoning, for the shack was occupied by *bandoleros* who opened fire on me as I approached.

On the run, I dived into a big vat, one of those used for washing coffee beans. Bullets were hitting around me like hail, and suddenly a grenade landed right on top of me. I seized it instantly and threw it back with all my stength, but it exploded very close by and some fragments wounded me in the leg. I could not see the *bandoleros* from the vat—which seemed likely to become my coffin—so as best I was able I climbed up to a drying rack, receiving in the process a carbine bullet, which went through my left arm.

Providentially, a mounted patrol hurried to my aid. The *bandoleros* took flight, leaving two of their number dead on the patio of the house. I joined the soldiers in pursuit of the *bandoleros*, who covered their retreat by hurling hand grenades at us, half a dozen in all.

I was seriously wounded; I felt my strength leaving me and I was bleeding profusely.

Two of the *bandoleros* tried to cross the Vieja River; I wanted to follow them, but I fell to the ground unconscious. I do not know how much time had elapsed before I regained my senses. At that moment I was aware of people talking and with great effort I managed to grasp a grenade and pull the pin, ready to throw it at the *bandoleros*.

Fortunately, I recognized the voice of the corporal of the patrol and I called to him to come and put the pin back in my grenade, because I did not have the strength to do so. Twice that day, then, I held death in my hands, in the form of a hand grenade.

I learned later that the patrol killed those who tried to escape across the river.

They radioed for helicopters and I was flown in a Kaman to Cartago, where the doctors stopped my bleeding, gave me shots and blood, and sent me to the hospital in Armenia.

37 · The Lady with the Light-Blue Eyes

Appearances are deceiving.

It was about an hour before midnight on Sunday, a normal Sunday. The night breeze tempered the rigors of the excessively hot weather of Cartago. In the outskirts of the colonial city was a pavillion, a place where people danced and drank and fought on fiesta days. Near the pavilion a woman was awaiting someone's arrival. An elegant woman, stylishly dressed in high heels and carrying a purse, she had blue eyes and her hair was meticulously arranged. A pair of tipsy strollers passed by her and made some brandy-inspired remarks, but their coarse suggestions failed to ruffle the lady's serenity. Brave indeed she must have been to wander the streets at that hour, alone, exposed to the abuse of criminals, drunks, and other undesirables.

"Why, you old bat," blurted out one rejected volunteer escort.

That lady, who did not smile, did not smoke, did not accept invitations to have a drink, much less allow herself to be pinched, had to be involved in some great intrigue.

When the bold occupants of a car got out and straightway moved toward her, she, frightened, turned and ran, disappearing between two buildings. In vain they followed her, because she agilely scaled a wall and vanished in the darkness.

Conrado Salazar used every means he could to find a way to eliminate me. One day Cabezón, a driver by profession, a very ill-tempered individual, mean and ugly, and a trusted agent for Conrado, located me—how I do not know—and he said confidentially to me:

"The chief wants to have a little talk with you. He wants you to come up to Riberalta to talk about reorganizing the *cuadrilla*. What you did in La Trocha was all right, because those that disobey get killed."

I stood there silent, waiting for Cabezón to finish speaking, trying to divine Conrado's intentions. I was ready to pull my gun if my interlocutor tried to attack me.

"Listen, Zarquito," he continued, "if you're afraid to go up to Riberalta, Conrado says for you to pick the place and the time, and he'll come down. The truth is the chief wants capable, tough men in the *cuadrilla*."

Was Zarpazo plotting my destruction or, on the other hand, might he be thinking that I could still be useful to him in his operations?

"Tell him all right," I responded. "If that's the way things are, I'm ready to work with him. Tell him to come to Cartago next Sunday an hour before midnight. I'll be waiting for him at the pavilion, on the Ansermanuevo Road side."

On the Sunday of the meeting, at the appointed hour, I waited for Conrado, hiding my impatience. There I was, in a wig and a fine dress, with make-up, including an application of eye-shadow and eye-liner that Sophia Loren would have envied; I suffered almost unbearable pain in my feet because of the high heels I was wearing. Two 8.6 mm. revolvers and fifty rounds of ammunition in the purse gave me the courage to wait for the *bandolero* and his companions. If Conrado showed up, I felt sure he would die. Not even a magician would have seen through my disguise of the evening. However those damned amorous riders pulled the cheese out of the trap. Under those circumstances I fled in order not to fall into the hands of those devotees of the evening drive, who were pursuing me as the fox pursues the hen, as the hawk pursues the dove, as old women thirst for cocoa. I, in flight and without breaking my stride, threw off wig, blouse, slippers and skirt.

Cabezón had succeeded in discovering my residence, and,

with fresh information on my activities, he returned to Conrado's camp. My life was now indeed in danger, for Zarpazo surely would not rest until he had me killed. But a soldier, once alerted, does not allow himself to be surprised!

38 · A First-Class Interment

Seek and ye shall find.

On December 16, 1964, the Colombian populace went to the polls to elect by democratic process the representatives to the Chamber, deputies, and certain local officials.

We of the military are not political partisans, but neither do we just watch the bulls from the fence. We go to the populous city or the rural precinct to guarantee the "free exercise of the ballot," as the political scientists say.

I was in Armenia, and my assignment differed from the routine. Late in the afternoon I entered a *cantina* through its half-closed door. I had the electoral ink on the index finger of my right hand and appeared to be just one of so many citizen voters. Some item of information might be picked up for the brigade on such an important day, at a moment of heightened political fervor, and at a place frequented by all classes of people.

In the *cantina*, which was located on the road to Montenegro, two ugly looking fellows were drinking liquor out of demitasse cups in an attempt to disguise their violation of the election-day ban. Since you cannot catch fish without throwing in the hook, pushing my hat back, I tilted back my head and shouted:

"*Viva* Rojas Pinilla!"

"*Viva* the Liberal Party!" they shouted back, rushing toward me.†

I side-stepped them and shouted: "Well, *viva* the Liberal Party, too!"

One of the pair left the *cantina*.

"*Viva* Rojas Pinilla!" I reiterated even more loudly.

The remaining man rushed at me with a knife in his right hand and a chair in the left—but he was staring into the barrel of my revolver. Whereupon he tossed aside his weapon and bellowed:

"We're going to be good friends!"

I asked the proprietor to close the door and open a bottle of liquor. There being no secrets in a bottle, my pigeon sang beautifully. He said that he had a cache of weapons, that I was a tremendous guy, that we could organize a *cuadrilla* of which I would be the chief and he my second in command. I went along with this line of talk and, when he was pretty high, we left the *cantina* together.

The man expressed himself well and seemed intelligent. We had walked a couple of blocks when he suddenly proposed a different plan of action:

"Say, after thinking it over, let's turn the guns over to the police and that way we'll get some money."

My native suspicion flashed a warning. There's something fishy about this, I thought.

"I know a lot about that kind of business," I replied. "The government of Valle is offering a reward for my head. You'd better come with me to my house. I want to pick up a pistol."

Talking all the while, I cunningly took him by taxi to a spot near brigade headquarters. Then I stuck my gun in his ribs and delivered him to the duty officer.

---

†The "*viva*" for (Gustavo) Rojas Pinilla, president from June, 1953, to May, 1957, was an attempt to draw out some action. Since Rojas Pinilla was beginning a comeback as a Conservative politician by late 1964, the answering "*vivas*" for the Liberal Party constituted a challenge to fight.

During the interrogation he had to repeat his statements about the guns cached away. As a result the brigade sent out a staff sergeant, me, and the suspect to bring back the arms.

At eight in the evening we were leaving Armenia in the truck I had at my disposal; at ten we were digging away with pick and shovel six paces from a big pole, in the middle of a *cafetal*, under the cover of darkness.

About ten feet down we found a double wooden box with a tin covering, which contained five rifles, eight uniforms, *carabinero* hats, leggings, boots, cartridge belts, and rifle ammunition.

The *bandolero* had been such a good informant that at La Montaña at midnight our men also dug up a large plastic bag full of ammunition.

We were leaving the *cafetal* with the recovered loot when they started shooting at us. I was carrying the ammunition on my back and was not able to do anything at the moment. However the sergeant drove off the attackers and saved the day.

At two in the morning we were reporting to the brigade commander on our successful mission.

On Maundy Thursday, with the new informant, I went to the settlement of La Española, where we recovered a San Cristóbal carbine and ammunition.

This ex-*bandolero* helped us a great deal with his information, which enabled the Mobile Group to make several surprise raids that broke up the *cuadrilla* of the dreaded Joselito.

39 · Tarzan, Zorro, and Conejo

Where and when you least expect it, up jumps the rabbit.

A lottery-ticket seller, a good informant, told brigade headquarters that there was a wounded *bandolero* near

Campanario. Having received this same information from three other sources, we had no doubt of its reliability.* The brigade commander ordered out a mission. On this occasion my partner was Corporal N.N., nicknamed "El Zorro" (the fox). (We used nicknames, as the *bandoleros* did, so that the civilians would not identify us as being of the military.)

We traveled toward Campanario, moving into mountainous country. To people we came in contact with I was "Tarzan" and the young ladies gave us their full attention.

The hours went by and we did not turn up any clue as to the location of the wounded man. Since time is money, in peace or in war, I decided to try something. I suggested to the corporal that he pretend to be ill; if this trick failed to produce information, we would return to Armenia.

I asked where I could find medical attention so Zorro could get a shot because he was ill. They told me the old fellow who did that sort of thing lived a long way from there.

"That doesn't matter," I answered.

At the end of two hours' drive I greeted Don José. I said that Zorro had a bad case of VD that was eating him up. Right away he gave him a shot, and shortly the corporal was tossing around on the cot and was vomiting up everything the generous people had urged upon him. His temperature went up to a hundred and four, and maybe higher. While we waited for the reaction to the shot to subside, Don José, who had accepted me as Tarzan, let it slip that he was treating a fellow called "Conejo" (rabbit), one of Sangrenegra's *cuadrilla*, recently wounded by soldiers.

"Zorro also belongs to the *cuadrilla* of Jacinto Cruz Usma, who was killed recently, and I'm picking up the stragglers," I told him. "How far away is the place where Conejo is?"

"Cross-country, about five hours," he replied.

---

*Information, or military intelligence, determines the success or failure of an action against *bandoleros*. Remember the maxim: "If you know yourself and you know your enemy, you can enter into battle under favorable circumstances."

Don José was the guide for the first part of the trip, which we started after dark. The good man begged me to try to bring Conejo back, because he was tired from traveling so far to treat him.

Don José had reason to be tired. To walk, just like that, ten hours every couple of days was not very appealing. "To be an infantryman is a good fate," but fatiguing.

After covering about ten miles we met a little old man at a house.

"Sangrenegra was here for two days before he died," he stated. "The troops passed by, up along there. He wouldn't shoot."

Don José left to go back home and the old man was our guide to another house, which we reached at seven in the morning.

A man there assured us Conejo was nearby, up in a cave among the rocks, and he went up to announce that Tarzan was waiting for him. Zorro and I stayed behind, ready to make our next move in case Conejo did not trust us.

The wounded man came down carrying a San Cristóbal carbine.

"Good morning, sir," he greeted me.

"Good morning, Conejo. Don't you remember me?"

"Sangrenegra's meetings with Tarzan were all at night; I don't really know."†

Conejo's strength revived with a good breakfast at the house. After the meal I ordered:

"Conejo, take the shells out of your carbine and wrap it in your *ruana*, and tie it well with this rope."

This was a simple precaution to make sure the rabbit would not turn into a tiger. We were about to start back when Conejo asked me:

"When are you coming back around here?"

"In about a week," I answered.

---

†Buitrago was deceiving the wounded *bandolero* with his alias "Tarzan," because a real *bandolero* with that alias had operated recently in the same region.

"Then I'll wait for you here. I feel weak and I can't travel."

I pretended to be angry and even hurt.

"Zorro, shoot this traitor," I commanded Corporal N.N. "There's a hundred and fifty thousand peso reward for me and this scum is going to hand me over to the *chulos*."

"Don't shoot me! I'll go with you . . . to show you I'm no squealer; I wouldn't betray you."

"If that's the way it is," I concluded, "then let's get moving!"

I went first, Conejo was next, and Corporal N.N. brought up the rear. We had the safeties off on our guns in case the young fellow tried some trick, or in case the *bandoleros* attacked. The sly lad knew more than we thought, for when we took a rest he revealed:

"Sangrenegra left some guns at Escobal, but he ordered me to take them to Páramo de Santa Elena. I gave them to Don José, the manager of the bathhouse. I'm the only one who can get them back."

Good, I thought, this is getting better.

We walked for six hours and finally came to the highway under construction that went to Planadas. We met a station wagon, which, under the circumstances, was like finding life itself. We were thoroughly tired.

Politely, I asked the driver to take us to Calarcá. He replied that he couldn't because he had to make a milk pickup right away.

Bound and gagged, the driver and his helper occupied the place for the milk cans in the rear, while Conejo, Zorro, and I climbed into the front. We stopped at the edge of Calarcá, and I sent a little girl over to summon the driver of a black car parked there.

"It is urgent that we get to Armenia."

The man looked at us and laconically responded: "All right. Let's go."

The milk was delivered late that day; as the black car carried us toward Armenia, the two milkmen lay bound in the station wagon we had abandoned.

Two blocks from brigade headquarters I asked: "How much do I owe you, sir?"

"Nothing."

"Thanks. If you look back or you ever say anything about this in Calarcá, I'll kill you."

We got out. The driver, startled and baffled, put the car in gear and drove off.

I told Conejo we were going to a house where they would give me fifteen thousand pesos, of which I would give him three thousand so he could buy clothes.

Opposite the brigade headquarters there was a military housing project. When Conejo saw the military vehicles he blurted:

"There are the *chulos*!"

He tried to run but we grabbed him.

"Don't make a fuss," hissed Zorro. "They'll shoot us if you do."

Conejo's expression of terror when we entered headquarters could better be painted than described.

"Take it easy now; make yourself at home." I added: "Now, come on and repeat what you told us along the way."

He was barely seventeen years old, and he was already caught up in the savagery of *la violencia*!

40 · More About the Same

The devil makes use of the repentent.

Seventy-two straight hours on the road will exhaust even the hardiest. Our bodies cried out for rest, but the brigade commander had declared that the immediate recovery of the gun cache was essential.

"Well, colonel," I said. "When there is work to be done, we do it. Let's not miss the opportunity, or they might get ahead of us all of a sudden."

Corporal N.N. was still under the weather because of the shot for VD.

Since the call of duty conforms to no schedule, we, overcoming our weariness, that same afternoon went to Ibagué. The party was composed of Major J.J., Sergeant-major R.R., Corporal V.V., Conejo, and me.

As the car was traveling up toward La Línea I thought about this martyred, outlying region, so scourged by the *bandoleros* for a decade and a half. The peace of God must return to the Quindío region, a land of promise, of amazing fertility, which compensates man a thousand fold. There would be peace in Caldas, Valle, and Tolima because it was an imperative for Colombia; we would secure it in open battle against the *bandoleros*, even if we had to certify it with our life's blood. Through my memory passed the recollection of so many companions in arms, sacrificed in defense of our institutions, in protecting our good citizens, and in pursuing violators of the law. So many heroes, who have filled the pages of the Orders of the Day, and who have left, as a reminder of their journey through this life, a citation and a medal.

"This is the commander of the Sixth Brigade," I said to Conejo in Ibagué. "Tell him all you know."

It was ten o'clock at night and Conejo, interned in the guardhouse, had refused to open his mouth. I had drilled it into him not to say anything without my consent. The completion of our missions required our being close-mouthed.

How many headaches we would be spared in the military if we all would watch our tongues and at times seal our lips. Sweetheart, family, friends—no one ought to know that we are going out on a particular mission, that we will carry out this or that operation. The walls have ears, and a simple indiscretion can result in a catastrophe. To conclude this, let me cite a verse of Scripture that is extremely appropriate here: "He who watches his tongue, guards his life; he who opens his lips often, will bring about his own ruin."

After noon on the next day, the executive officer of the Roock Battalion took us to Juntas, where a combat task force was training for its forthcoming move to Marquetalia. In Juntas the major briefed Colonel P.P., commander of the Roock Battalion, on the situation and our mission. Then a lieutenant drove the rest of us as far as the road leading off to the spa. The people who had come there to bathe in the warm springs were frightened by our arrival, but the lieutenant calmed them by telling them to trust us, that we were four noncoms dressed in civilian clothes.

Before arriving at the bathhouse, whose proprietor was the custodian of the arms cache, I said to Conejo:

"Tell Don José that I am Zarpazo, the new chief, and that I have come to pick up the guns." I could not say I was Tarzan because the manager was acquainted with that *bandolero*.

"Good afternoon, Conejo," said a man who approached us.

"Good afternoon. How are you, Don José?" replied Conejo, and he added: "This is Zarpazo, the new chief."

With this introduction, I immediately stated the reason for my presence to Don José: "I've come for those guns."

"There are a lot of people around at the springs and that would be dangerous."

"It's all right. I've already told them we were four noncoms in civvies. And you, if they ask you, tell them the same."

The manager left us for a moment and returned with cigarettes. He said to us confidentially:

"Those boobs out there swallowed that story about you being soldiers. We don't need to worry."

At about four o'clock there appeared a young man, sent by the manager to take us to Páramo de Santa Elena. He informed us that Don José would reach the same spot by a different route.

After covering some ten miles we reached our destination which Conejo recognized, and there found Don José in the company of three men.

"There's Sinsonte, Turpial, and Oso, from Sangrenegra's old gang," said Conejo to me, and then he restated our purpose. Don José was obviously perplexed because the three *bandoleros* were claiming for themselves the same guns that we had come for.

"You have to give the guns to me because I'm the one who brought them," declared Conejo.

As if by magic the hidden treasure came forth from among the rocks: an automatic rifle, a .45-caliber Kiraly carbine (from the national police), four Mauser rifles, two hundred ten cartridges, and seven magazines—enough to stage a first-class ambush.

The three *bandoleros* eyed the arsenal enviously, but we had our weapons ready just in case. I made a veiled suggesttion to the trio that they join me in an attack on the military post at Juntas (with the idea of handing them over as prisoners), but those wily foxes smelled a trap and took advantage of the approaching darkness to disappear.

"That's the way they are," Conejo commented. "Yellow. Sangrenegra kicked them out for being cowards."

When we returned to the Roock Battalion with the guns the commander evidenced his satisfaction with the outcome of the mission.

In Armenia we saluted the colonel with a report of "mission accomplished."

Conejo had become an extremely helpful informant, and he helped us recover uniforms, vehicles, and other equipment belonging to the military forces. This young man turned honest, and at the present time he is loyally serving the army and, consequently, his country. May heaven help him continue thus, for the old saying contains the experience of centuries when it observes: "A firebrand, though once extinguished, easily lights again."

4l · In a Café in Armenia

The fight is in the fighting.

That Saturday, as was the rule on the weekends, the Café Nuevo Mundo in Armenia was packed.

An informant hastened to the brigade headquarters with the warning that there were *bandoleros* among the crowd at said establishment. This news was serious because it indicated that the *bandoleros* were armed.

Three noncoms were ordered to the café to check out the report and, if it proved correct, to capture the criminals. We three wore street clothes.

"Three beers, doll. Three Pokers—and right away. It's mighty thirsty out tonight."

As we savored the fine flavor and the foam evaporated from the "grain juice," we focused our attention on a large table where four suspicious looking men were about to leave with a girl they had picked up. These men were, in fact, the *bandoleros*, right there in the center of Armenia, trying once more to defy the authorities, emboldened by their prior crimes, making a show of bluff and bluster.

The fight would not be equal—three against four. We stood up with feigned casualness, and as I went to the restroom my companions strolled in the direction of the door of the café.

One of the *bandoleros* walked out to the street where one of the noncoms tried to arrest him. A shot rang out and the noncom who was standing in the doorway pitched forward, apparently wounded. With a leap I landed in the midst of the fight. The *bandoleros* greeted me with flying lead, but I fired my revolvers even faster and with greater accuracy. The leader of the quartet fell dead and one of the others was wounded. The last man fled in the confusion.

The quartet had been operating around La Tebaida, quite at will and so cleverly that complete information about their location and activities had not come to us. Their crimes, however, were so serious in nature that the government of Valle was offering a 15,000-peso reward for the man who had been killed. The corporal we thought to be wounded fortunately got up safe and sound.

Mission accomplished. Noncoms, back to the barracks.

A few days after the incident, some moneybags from Le Tebaida showed up at brigade headquarters with the intention of rewarding with cold cash the person who had killed the *bandolero*.

The informant was rewarded, as a matter of fact. We noncoms, however, remained anonymous, a policy in the best interests of society and the operation of the brigade.

But our reward was better than money; it was the satisfaction of having done our duty!†

42 · Behind Bars

Mister Policeman, I didn't say anything.

"Hands up!" the sergeant of the guard of the Armenia police ordered me. "Search him," he added, to his guards. "Take his watch, jewelry, and money. It will all be returned when he leaves."

"Take the laces out of your shoes and give us your belt. We don't want you to decide to hang yourself . . . and be 'spirited' out of our jail."

The cell to which they led me was not large enough to

---

†Readers who take offense at Buitrago's egoism and constant moralizing about duty should know that none of the Colombian gang infiltrators, all of them noncoms on modest salary, ever accepted a reward for catching a *bandolero*, and none is known ever to have kept any of the recovered bandit money or booty. Perhaps this is what was meant when Gonzalo Canal Ramírez, Colombia's leading interpreter of civil-military relations, told me: "Our military men have been a special breed of heroes, perhaps saints."

permit me to lie down. From the rough cement walls seeped a nauseating stench produced by an accumulation of assorted filth and grime saturated with urine. The dark cell was secured by a metal door with a little window in the upper part, well above eye level for me. The cells were located under the baths, and consequently the intense moist cold made us shiver continually. All this was complemented by the voracity of the bedbugs that clung to one's neck and back and produced unbearable, foul sores.

The fact that it was fiesta-time in Armenia made it necessary for all avilable law officers to be on duty to maintain order throughout the city. As a result, from the time I entered the pokey, at two in the afternoon, until morning of the next day no guard appeared to bring me food or to let me out to relieve myself.

To think that I had been in service eight years without ever having been in jail, without ever having been put on report, without every having been arrested.

Not being able to sleep, I meditated, and through an association of ideas I recalled the words of a Mexican song, very popular in every greasy spoon that had a jukebox:

This will be my song behind bars,
sad as a sigh, as a lament.
This will be my spirit's last pain,
before they take me to the cemetery.

At dawn they brought us bread and coffee and took us to the toilet. A few minutes later we were back in our dungeons.

About ten o'clock the jailer-corporal appeared, jangling a bunch of keys, a signal that we were about to have a few minutes in the open air. There were not many of us in the cells—a marijuana user, two pansies, a sneak thief, and two criminal suspects.

Suddenly the pothead, high on the accursed weed, attacked the jailer, but the guards subdued him with a blow from a rifle butt. Then, as if the rest of the prisoners had had something to do with the incident, they decided to "allow" us to give vent to our animus through exercise—calisthenics, push-ups, sprints, laps around the yard.

"That guy must have had some training," the jailer said, referring to me.

"Indeed I have, corporal!"

"Where were you in service?"

"In the *llanos*."

"Do you have your service record?"

"Negative, corporal. I don't carry papers with me; they're at home."

"Well, where do you live?"

"I came from Sonsón, Antioquia, with my uncle, who probably has some of my papers."

At this point the aforementioned marijuana smoker, bored with the interrogation that was taking place, insulted the corporal's mother and then there was the devil to pay! The irate commander of the guard rushed into the melee, giving kicks right and left.

The corporal tried to explain that I had been exercising properly and was not involved. The sergeant muttered an obscenity and stalked off.

Then, possibly so the bedbugs could slake their thirst, we were made to wash down the cells, being chained and well guarded all the while.

As if to assist us to achieve a proper religious state through fasting, they gave us no noon meal.

At four in the afternoon a police corporal brought us bread and water. On opening the door of my cell he said: "Here, take this."

I recognized him by his voice first and then by his face. He had gone on patrol duty with me at the military post in Balboa. He was an excellent *carabinero* and a good man in fighting the *bandoleros*. Whenever they ordered me to carry out some difficult assignment I always took him with me, just as I always took Francisco A. Bustamante—serial number 15-05, if I remember correctly—a brave, capable man who fell heroically in a surprise attack against the *cuadrilla* led by José María Osorio, alias Joselito.

"What the devil are you doing here, sergeant?" he asked me.

"Well, I'll tell you, friend," I replied. "But talk quietly."

After the greeting and handshakes, I set about recounting what had happened to me and in the telling I was temporarily transported from my dungeon.

"Right now I am operating out of uniform," I told him, "in the performance of certain duties for the brigade. I was talking with a girl in the Café Renobar and enjoying my beer when she said to me in a frightened voice: 'Here come the F-2 men. Go out through that door, go up the steps and go out through the apartments.'

"Previously I had noted that a politician there, who knew me as a *pájaro* [a lone bandit, not belonging to any band], had been looking at me with a fixed stare. At the time I did not think this would become a serious matter.

"To avoid revealing my identity, I lit out for the stairs. The F-2 men in street clothes, already spotted in the café by the girl, pulled their guns on me. Another move and they would have shot me.

"Considering my appearance, I had everything against me: long sideburns, a Beatles haircut, *ruana*, sombrero, drill trousers, a loud striped shirt, and Carmelite sandals. Since I carried no papers but did pack two revolvers, in the eyes of the diligent men of F-2, I had to be some kind of criminal. I was relieved of my weapons and a belt with eighty rounds and then led handcuffed to the police jail.

"There I gave a false name, of course, and in the blotter they booked me as a suspicious character. And that's the story."

"Buitrago, why didn't you say so in the first place? This unpleasantness could have been avoided," exclaimed the major, Commandant of Police of Armenia.

"I simply could not do it, Major," I responded.

"One man coming out!" shouted the Corporal of the Guard, so the sentry would allow me to depart.

At brigade headquarters they laughed until they could laugh no more about my two-day adventure, or rather, misadventure.

43 · Ñato Armendaris

*Honor demands more from the soldier than from
the martyr; it demands that he work, that he fight
and that he be victorious.*

Violence is the most terrible scourge a civilized country
can face—so we are told in the book *De la violencia a la paz*
("From Violence to Peace"), edited by the Command of the
8th Brigade.

Those of us who, for reasons well known to these readers,
have had to take an active part in *la violencia* know about its
ramifications, its demoniacal connections, its conflicting
interests, which render to it a tribute of blood, pain, and
tears.

In this chapter I wish to recall something that happened
in the capital of the Quindío, by whose undesirable element I
was considered to be a complete and thoroughgoing *bandolero*.

On a certain occasion a man of considerable wealth and
importance, whom they called "Ñato" (to which I shall add
the name Armendaris because he was from Armenia), made
this "business proposition" to me:

"Man, I got to tell you something. You're one tough
hombre! Now, we need to have some troublesome people
from Armenia disposed of. We'll give you ten thousand pesos
for killing Dr. X., and twenty thousand for killing Dr. N.N.
and Mr. X.X."

"It's a deal," I answered. "I'll get rid of them for you.
But give me three thousand as a little down payment to cover
my expenses while I'm doing the job!"

He handed me a check and the deal was closed.

By the fastest means available, I alerted the intended victims and arranged for F-2 to provide continuing protection.
After a week I returned to Ñato to explain the delay, declar-
ing that I was ill.

"Here's a fellow that'll go with you," Ñato declared, indicating a certain Misac, who was such a fine fellow the government of Caldas was offering five thousand pesos for him.

Pretending to be friends, Misac and I went about the city with the object of carrying out "orders." I was hopeful we would not encounter any of the "condemned" men, but at the same time I knew my presence assured they would not be villainously assassinated; I would never permit it.

Since the encounter never occurred, Ñato changed his order. He told us that at a certain hour every day a *carabinero* from the Pantanillo post went alone to visit his sweetheart. Our mission was clear: kill this policeman and take his weapons.

As we were traveling to the spot where we would set up ambush, I thought about the National Police, an institution that has fought ardently for Colombia by the side of the military forces. How many vigils, how many nights spent in endless waiting, how many harsh hours endured for the sake of establishing order in city and countryside, often receiving as recompense abuse, hardship, and even death—and in addition, a lack of comprehension and appreciation on the part of the very people they were protecting.†

Alfred de Vigny was right when he said that the most beautiful thing, after inspiration, is sacrifice. Of course good Colombians—and they are many—know how important the National Police is for the peace of the country, for its safety, and for its progress.

We were watching the aforementioned *carabinero*, who, riding on a docile mule and innocently oblivious, was approaching the house of his sweetheart. We all make mistakes, because we are human, but to ride out alone in an uninhabited stretch with a San Cristóbal carbine, was simply suicide. He was not doing so through lack of experience, much less lack of instruction, but rather drawn by that magnet called

---

†While the National Police have indeed been blamed unfairly, by irresponsible partisan spokesmen, for alleged abuses in certain law-enforcement actions, it is equally true that National Police elements participated in numerous illegal acts of repression and murder between 1946 and 1953.

love, which is more powerful than the gods or death.

"I'll kill him," Misac resolutely announced. He moved forward a few paces, seeking the best target, but I softly called to him. "What's the matter?" he asked.

"I heard somebody take the safety off a rifle," I whispered, hoping that with this lie the seconds would pass and the *carabinero* would safely pass.

"This guy is coming and I'm not going to wait," he answered as he stealthily moved up behind a tree and cocked his revolver. My conscience considered this choice: the *carabinero* or the *bandolero*—the guardian of order or the consummate offender?

There was no time for philosophizing. My machete came from its sheath at this juncture and flashed through the air.

The enamored *carabinero* passed by, tranquilly, unaware of the incident he had occasioned.

"Hasn't Misac shown up? He told me to wait for him while he went to see an old girl friend. He kept me waiting so long I came on back. We'll have to take care of our business next week!"

"That's the way that so-and-so is," observed Ñato. "He has done this to me several times now. Nowadays you just can't depend on anybody."

44 · More with Ñato

A thief who steals from a thief receives a hundred days' pardon.

"Do you know 'Puente Roto'?" Armendaris asked me on another occasion.

"Sure, I do! You know, he's a good friend of mine," I replied slyly.

"I want you to deliver to him fifty rifle cartridges, which he urgently needs. Do you know where El Mesón is, a tavern in Cartago?"

"Who doesn't?" I answered.

"Well, this is pretty dangerous. There are several military detachments around, and they search everybody; and they'd just as soon shoot you as not."

"If that's what I have to do, I'll die, but some of them will die first."

Later in a machine shop I was given fifty cartridges—.30 caliber, brand new—and fifty pesos for expenses. At five o'clock the following morning I was traveling in a Flota Occidental bus on the way to Pereira. From there I continued by Trejos express bus to Cartago. I had noted on my departure from Armenia I was being followed by a suspicious looking man. I wondered whether he might be a DAS agent or an F-2 man, and I was uneasy, but on thinking it over I said to myself:

"If he's a secret agent and he searches me, all the better, since the cartridges definitely will end up at brigade headquarters. If they put me in jail, Ñato has good lawyers and I won't be cooling my heels in jail very long. Nobody need know I am a noncom."

I had breakfast and was leaving the hotel in Cartago when I met face to face the man who had been following me.

"You've been tailing me since I left Armenia," I declared. "What do you want with me?"

"Ñato ordered me to go along with you. I'm Toño."

"Show me the countersign so I'll know."

He pulled out a card that had a red ribbon fastened to it and bore the signature of Armendaris.

"If you hadn't shown me that and fast, I'd have blasted you, because I suspected you were fuzz."

We kept up a conversation until we reached El Mesón.

A plan had been worked out the day before, involving certain noncoms from the San Mateo and Vencedores battalions, dressed in street clothes. They knew me and were to help me in the capture of Puente Roto.

When I passed by them I recognized them, but my companion scarcely noticed the three men working on a car.

We had been waiting for three hours in El Mesón when a lad with a message finally appeared. "Leave," the note read.

"Someone is waiting for you at the Café Ganadero." I couldn't speak to the agents without risking disclosure of our plan. So, betraying no emotion but meditating on my annoyance, I went to the café specified. There in the flesh was Ñato.

"That other fellow couldn't come because he is sick," he explained, excusing the absence of Puente Roto.

"What you're doing is playing games with me," I replied with severity. "If you are not satisfied with my work, I'm leaving. To hell with this!"

"Come on, now, Mono; don't get hot under the collar. It's not my fault. I'm going to prove it to you now with some real action!"

At the end of a brief ride in a station wagon we entered the house of a lawyer, near Bolívar Park. I was introduced to the host as "one of us" and was invited to sit down to lunch. Then they introduced a tall, thin man who emerged from a nearby room; he identified himself as "El Duende" (the ghost), and truly he expressed himself spiritedly. He told me that he had an experienced band near Villa Rodas and that if I wanted to join there were good possibilities for making a few pesos.

"I've had better offers," I answered. "I prefer to kill people in town. I don't like taking to the woods where the soldiers can track you. I've already done the *cuadrilla* bit."

Ñato Armendaris, who had been sitting silently, pulled a hundred and fifty cartridges for a San Cristóbal carbine out of a suitcase and handed them, together with five thousand pesos in loose bills, to El Duende. The latter, very satisfied with this presentation, faded out of the picture.

All that had happened I reported to my superiors and showed them the shiny cartridges. They ordered me to continue with the assignment. "He who wants something will have to pay something," I quoted to myself mentally, as I went about locating Ñato. I found him in a brothel, where he had a girl. From such environments comes information that may prove very useful, if one knows how to take advantage of the liquor-loosened tongues of the clients, and if one has the knack of gaining the confidence of prostitutes, newsboys, bootblacks, lottery salesmen—people who, because of their type of work, are in contact with the lowest strata of society.

"Leave the ammunition here and instead take care of that little business in Armenia," Ñato said cordially. He gave me a thousand pesos and took the cartridges to the toilet, where he hid them.

Since we were in the *cantina* of the house of ill fame, I pretended to get drunk. When Ñato departed for the other accommodations with his girl friend, I moved to the toilet, where I found the ammunition; then hiding it under my *ruana*, I returned to my table and pretended to be asleep.

An hour after midnight Ñato came in grumbling: "You're drunk! Go sleep it off."

For a reply I waved my revolver in the air and fired it three times. Infuriated, Armendaris shoved and kicked me to the door. On the street I doubled around several blocks and then walked to brigade headquarters, where I delivered the cartridges.

"What do you think, Mono, about the ammunition being stolen? It must have been that girl . . . or who knows?"

"I feel sure the thief was Toño, the fellow that trailed me to Cartago. When I was pretty well drunk that night, I saw him go into the john and then he came running out. Besides, I've seen him at the F-2 office. I don't know whether he's trying to put something over on us. I don't like anything about this. Keep in mind, now, if you two are trying to pull something on me, I'll kill you and the devil himself."

"I'll pay you two thousand pesos to beat up Toño," offered Ñato.

"We'll see."

This "mission" was unnecessary because Toño was no longer of this world. The police had killed him.

45 · The Price of Murder

*War is a conflict of interests with a bloody reso-
lution.*

The first potter's field was paid for with Christ's blood,
and the clink of those thirty pieces of silver has echoed
through the centuries as a reminder of the most infamous of
all betrayals.

During *la violencia*, haciendas were bought at low prices,
as a result of the killing off of entire families or the slaughter
of honest landowners. The heirs, "persuaded" by the terrify-
ing carnage, were obliged practically to give away their land—
to abandon fields lovingly tilled by generations.† A horrible
business, fruit of the avarice of certain men with insatiable
appetities, who always want more and more, worshippers of
their own bellies, whose banner is food and whose aspiration
is sufficiency.

"Things are fouled up," Ñato remarked to me. "There are
a lot of stool pigeons around and you can't accomplish anything. Take this card and go to Calcarcá; there's a Señor
Lopijo there and he probably can use you. I don't want you
to get killed on me here in Armenia."

In Calcarcá, I found the man I sought. The card opened
wide for me the doors of his house; we chatted about everything, but Lopijo was always a little vague about things.

"I have to go to Cali, Don Félix [let us call him that].
I'll come back later."

The old man, in an overwhelming display of generosity
and a demonstration of his confidence in me, gave me five
hundred pesos. Then, having determined the coast was clear,
he began to speak quite openly:

"I need to have eight Conservatives killed . . . at El Para-

---

†During the 1960s the Colombian Supreme Court of Appeals issued
several rulings which withdrew legal sanction from ownership of
property acquired by fraud or intimidation during *la violencia*. Many
who could afford the litigation had their property restored to them.

guay, a settlement in Caicedonia . . . maybe their relatives then will sell me the farms cheap."

"For fifty thousand I'd be glad to, señor Lipijo. You know how tough things are!"

As I passed through Armenia, I notified brigade headquarters of the unusual proposition; then I continued to Cali, where I stayed two weeks because I was ill. On returning to Calcarcá I asked the old man:

"And how do I make sure you'll pay me after I do this little job for you?"

"An agreement is an agreement, Mono. You do the work and I'll pay. Go study the terrain around that settlement and we'll talk more later."

"You're right, Don Félix."

I shook his hand and set out on the road to El Paraguay.

"What are you going to do up here all by yourself, sergeant?" This question came from one of the brigade's informants, who managed a farm in the settlement.

"I'm not alone," I replied. "The others are at a stakeout. By the way, do you know old man Lopijo from Calcarcá?"

"I don't know him personally," answered the informant, "but I know that several neighboring landowners from here won a law suit from him over their property lines and that the old man swore to have them killed."

"We have that information, too," I told him. "We've come up here to help them."

I showed him the list of those "condemned" by Lopijo, but I did not mention my conversations with him.

"Yes, the information is correct. But there's no need for you to stay around, sergeant. The alerted soldier does not die in war. Those people will take care of themselves, I can assure you.

"Well, if that's the way things stand then I'll go."

Back in Calcarcá I walked into Don Félix's store and announced that I had reconnoitered the region and the best approaches were thus and so, and the people were such and such.

"Indeed now, Monito. I can see you have really been there and are taking an interest in your work."

"There's one problem," I suggested. "I need ammo for a San Cristóbal carbine."

"Well, that's no problem, Mono."

With that he squatted down and pulled from under his bed a sack of Aguila Roja coffee and from it took a hundred cartridges. What a precautious old man!

"Fine, don Félix. Now just wait for the wipe-out."

"How many are you going to need to help you in this?"

"That's not your concern. I'll kill them for you, and that will be that. Just have the money ready by the end of the week."

"By the end of the week . . . no. I don't have the money."

"That's the way I like it, Don Félix. You talk frankly. When you have the money let me know, and the next day I'll get rid of those people for you."

"Then, Mono, give me back the ammunition."

"I've got it in my hands now. Suppose I kill them now and give you a little time to get the money."

A week later an MK-2 grenade was tossed into Lopijo's house; he and his wife were wounded and a son was killed. I went to see him, hoping to find out who had done this crime, but it was obvious that he wasn't glad to see me. He called his wife and one of his sons and whispered something to them. Thereupon mother and son went out to the street.

This old devil has sent for the police, I thought to myself. So, addressing him I said: "I'm going out to get some cigarettes. I'll be back."

"Don't be long, Mono," he called after me.

I stood watching at the corner. My supposition was confirmed by the arrival of several policemen, who surrounded the house, revolvers in hand. Without waiting any further, I took off.

From Armenia, I sent Don Félix a letter:

Don Félix: You tricked me in our business deal and you called the law in on me. But just you wait; I have hands, too, and the world is very small. You will hear from me again soon.

The old man left Calarcá, and I turned the ammunition over to brigade headquarters.

46 · Sedalana

The monkey knows which limb to step on.

The new victim selected by the extortionists was the owner of the Almacén Sedalana, a department store in Armenia, right in the center of the city.

The extortion note was quite clear: twelve thousand pesos "or else."

The sad historical pattern in the Quindío made it necessary to consider the threat real. The money, wrapped in blue paper, was to be placed at eight that very night at the base of a large tree in Fundadores Park.

The park being new, everybody in Armedia, young and old, went there to stroll along its flower bordered paths.

Our mission was to find the extortionist, capture him, and recover the money.

Together with a corporal 1st class, I strolled around the park. We contacted a friend who had a house some fifty yards from the delivery spot, and he gave us permission to use his roof as an observation post.

At eight o'clock sharp Señor Sedalana rode up on a motorbike, got off and propped up the vehicle, and placed the blue package at the base of the tree. Five minutes later a figure wrapped in a *ruana* bent down and picked up the parcel. The corporal loosed a burst of submachine gun fire at the figure who, untouched, dashed away. Seeing that the trap was sprung, I gave a great leap from the low roof and pursued the fleeing figure. I fired a few shots into the air, so as not to kill or wound any of the many innocent people that filled the streets. Suddenly the fugitive fell, thus giving the corporal and me time to capture him. The man and the money ended up at brigade headquarters.

It seemed that the name Sedalana had some particular attraction, because a week later this same gentleman received another extortion note, this one upping the price by three thousand pesos. The fifteen thousand pesos were to be left in a vacant lot on 15th Street, between 12th and 13th avenues, at ten-thirty that very night.

The brigade planned a new operation. "Let me take charge of this," I asked the colonel.

At seven in the evening, with two corporals in a brand new station wagon, I made a reconnaissance of the terrain. At eight we returned to the lot, one at a time. Each of us lay down and covered himself with shavings that had been dumped there from a carpenter's shop. Even if someone had decided to examine the lot with a high-powered lantern he would never have discovered us. Without moving, we waited for whatever was to happen.

At ten-thirty sharp Señor Sedalana drove by in a Volkswagen and tossed out a package, which coincidentally fell right in our midst.

At almost the same instant a person was furtively making his appearance in search of the money. The readers will have guessed the outcome.

We led the cuprit, well handcuffed, to brigade headquarters, where there was nothing for him to do but confess his crime and name his confederates.

Since then, apparently, the wealthy department-store owner has not been bothered again.

47 · Cards on the Table

He who has more saliva can eat more flour.

To Señor Hugo Alvares (to you personally): We urgently need a hundred thousand pesos which is nothing to you. If you don't pay us we will kidnap your twin sisters.

Thus began a letter sent by parties unknown to a wealthy hacienda owner of the city of Armenia. Quite properly, he hastened to 8th Brigade headquarters to ask for help.

The colonel ordered me and another noncom to serve as Don Hugo's bodyguards—not just ordinary ones but as very dangerous *bandoleros*. Dress, gestures, ways of talking, we were quite familiar with all of this, so we could do it.

We gained the confidence of those who worked at Don Hugo's, the good workers and the bad. One day, during the coffee harvest, we started to speak ill of our employer:

"To come so far to watch out for this miserable old geezer! I feel like kidnapping him myself."

That night one of the workers cautiously approached us. "If you are willing, we can do a piece of business."

"How's that?"

"We can't kidnap the old man, but we can get his twin sisters, and he thinks the world of them."

"Well, the first thing we ought to do is demand money," I said. "Let's threaten him, and if that doesn't work then we can do the kidnapping."

"If you like," the young man suggested. "I can write the letter."

"All right, do it, but do it right. Another thing—who can be counted on here? No stool pigeons . . ."

"We can only trust four of us," he stated. "You two, myself, and my brother."

"Aha! Well, the four of us will do some beautiful things. You get to work on the letter."

He wrote up the message.

"Fine," I said. "In a little while you slip it under the old man's door. You'll see that he'll give in, because if he doesn't, he's got real trouble."

We two agents slept in the room with Don Hugo. At four in the morning we found the letter; we opened it and in the presence of Don Hugo compared it with the first one. The form, the spelling, and the handwriting were the same.

"Let's go along with this for a while," we counseled.

Don Hugo called all his workers together and told them about the letter. He was ready to pay the money in order to save the lives of his sister, he said, but he hoped to heaven none of his workers were involved in the matter, because he would kill them, even if he had to go to jail for it.

That afternoon, the brothers came to say that they were going away because they had received a telegram saying their mother was very ill. The fact was, they were frightened by Don Hugo's threats.

"You guys want to pull a fast one on us," my companion shouted. "You want to squeal on us and get us killed."

We grabbed them and tied them up so vigorously and unexpected that they could not react. "Let's take them down to the river and kill them, the squealers," I said.

"Look, we're not squealers," they whined. "We're the same as you. You know, we were in on the holdup when they were paying the workers at the hacienda La Florida."

"So, there's some of that, too? Well, all nicely tied up you are going to brigade headquarters to repeat what you have just told us."

We carred them to Armenia in Don Hugo's car. Thus, with a little bit of ingenuity, we managed to uncover the ones involved in a holdup at a nearby hacienda, as well as those who were trying to extort a hundred thousand pesos.

48 · A Kidnapping

In guerrilla warfare initiative plays a decisive role.

There is nothing more repugnant to an honest person, to a true Christian, than a kidnapping. All human wretchedness is incarnate in that abominable act, which combines blackmail with treachery, cowardice with threat, extortion with piracy, bribery with indulgence. The death penalty, with charges, the reading of the sentence and the rolling of the drum, is not enough for those who, lacking all moral feeling, dedicate themselves to this infernal pursuit.

"Sergeant Buitrago, this is Don Juan," the brigade commander addressed me one day. "He has received this letter."

> Don Juan: we have kidnapped your son for whom you must bring us seventy thousand pesos and you will do it as we order.
>
> On the train from Pereira to Armenia take a seat on the right hand side of the coach. Between Alcalá and Quimbaya you will see the green coat your son was wearing and at that spot you will throw the money from the train. Mark well; you have twenty-four hours and do not notify the authorities, because if you do, the worst might happen.

The reader can imagine the anguish of the father, who was ready to obtain the money by selling his crops, his house—whatever was necessary to pay the ransom for his seventeen-year-old son. But what if, after he paid the money, his son were found dead? Can one accept the word of kidnappers? With what fervor Don Juan's prayers must have ascended to heaven at that most critical moment of his existence.

The colonel, the major, and I planned the operation.

"Don Juan," I said, "get the seventy thousand pesos ready and be waiting for us at six tomorrow morning at the train in Pereira."

At four in the morning, three of us noncoms, in street

clothes, were strolling through the designated station.

"Who's the engineer?" I asked the stationmaster.

A few minutes later we were having a cup of coffee with the engineer. I showed him the kidnapper's letter and explained who we were, whereupon he offered his complete cooperation. "What do you suggest, sergeant?"

"You know the signal for Don Juan to toss off the money. If you see the coat on the right side, let us know by giving one whistle; if it's on the left side, give two whistles. If you can, slow down a little when you whistle. We're going to jump off the train on the side opposite the coat. That way the train will hide us. Incidentally, here comes the father of the kidnapped boy. I want you to meet him."

We had no need for further conversation. At the proper time we got on the train and at seven it pulled out, carrying us on a mission filled with adventure and danger.

"Don Juan, keep your eyes open. As soon as you see the coat, throw the money off. Keep your window open. That's all you have to do."

One of the pleasures to be enjoyed by those who are in no hurry is traveling by train. It is interesting to study the faces of the passengers, to listen to their conversations, to feel the swaying of the coaches, to hear the jubilant whistle of the locomotive announcing the approaching station, to lean out the window and look at the S's formed by the curving string of cars, to contemplate the charm of the haciendas, the banana trees loaded with stalks, the coffee trees with their growing fruit.

When we passed through Alcalá, I alerted the other two noncoms and we stationed ourselves on the platform, next to the steps, ready to jump.

A little more than two miles from Quimbaya, the whistle blew once. The package of money sailed through the window.

"Let's go to the left, I shouted, and we leaped into space as the train hurtled along.

Fortunately, I landed beside a coffee tree and near a clump of banana trees, just a short distance from the money.

"Sergeant," whispered one of the noncoms, "I'm here; my buddy here has a bone broken in his hand."

"What shape are you in?"

"I'm all right . . . a little scratched up."

"Good," I answered. "The two of us will do what we can."

We were well camouflaged, watching, our weapons in hand. After ten minutes of tense waiting, three men appeared, armed with revolvers and wearing handkerchiefs over their nose and mouth. They were moving along opposite our position as they drew near the package.

Our crisp order, "Hands up!," took them by surprise. They wanted to react but they couldn't, so they threw down their guns and raised their hands.

"Where is the boy?" we anxiously asked the one who appeared to be the leader.

"We don't know anything about any boy," he replied.

"The one you kidnapped, Don Juan's son."

Time was passing, and there was a likelihood that confederates might come to the aid of these three, or that, because these were late in returning, those who were guarding the boy might kill him.

"Where's the boy?" I asked again, putting my gun close to the *bandolero*.

"I don't know what you're talking about," he answered, insolently. Then he made a quick grab for one of my revolvers, but he did not succeed. A sure shot left him lying quietly dead beside the seventy thousand pesos he had coveted.

With this, another criminal ran for the coffee trees, but he fell, wounded by our fire.

"Don't kill me," implored the third. "I'll tell you where the boy is. He's up the hill, a little over a quarter of a mile from here. My wife is guarding him. He's tied to an orange tree."

Following the *bandolero*, we hurried to the spot described. The woman had fled on hearing the shots, but the boy was unharmed.

With the joy that comes with victory, we listened to the account of the rescued youth as we walked back toward the highway. The anguish of the preceding evening was erased by the jubilation over the rescue. The embrace of the reunited father and son was the only (but the best!) reward for us, who had not hesitated in leaping from a speeding train so that a citizen might live.

I might add that Don Juan received intact his package of seventy thousand pesos and that, with the capture of one of the members and the death of two others, a gang of kidnappers that had plagued the region for a long time was eliminated.

49 · Electrician

My occupation? Whatever is needed!

A hacienda owner in the Quindío received a letter demanding thirty thousand pesos or else he would be killed. The man notified 8th Brigade headquarters, and on Wednesday three noncoms were assigned to the hacienda. Two went disguised as technicians from the Federación de Cafeteros, and I as an electrician.

According to the letter the hacienda owner was to hand over the money on Saturday, payday at the *finca*.

In my determination to appear the authentic electrician, I fear I disrupted completely the operation of the electric plant, for I hadn't the remotest idea of such operations.

Thursday and Friday the place was a beehive of activity. At about eleven on Saturday the owner was getting ready to pay the workers, and the technicians from the Federación were waiting in line with their tool kits in hand. At this point two mean-looking characters appeared, armed with revolvers, which they immediately pulled on the owner.

"Did you bring the money, old man?" they asked. At a signal from me the two technicians drew from their tool kits submachine guns and got the drop on the extortionists, who put up no resistance and were taken prisoner.

As it had been prearranged, one of the noncoms asked to see my papers, then they searched me and took my revolvers.

"If you guys are so tough," I challenged, "give me a gun and let's start shooting."

The electrician was handcuffed together with the *bandoleros*. Thus I gained their confidence and they felt no hesitancy in telling me that the *mayordomo* of the *finca* was the one who had put them up to the plot.

When we reached Armenia the noncoms reported to Major X.X. that I was a rebellious type and that I had offered to shoot it out with them.

"We will have to get rid of this blue-eyed joker," said the major.

The stick-up men ended up in jail, where that rascal the *mayordomo* joined them a few hours later.

50 · Puente Roto

An enemy surprised is already defeated.

Police agents sent information to 8th Brigade concerning the whereabouts of the *bandolero* Puente Roto, and preparations were made to send a detail under the command of Sergeant M.M. I did not think the information was very clear, and I told the commander so: "Colonel, I ask that I not be sent on this mission. It's a wild-goose chase." As I had anticipated, the mission returned without having found anyone.

The next day, however, an informant came in with some very precise data. "Now *that's* a mission I'd like to go on," I told the colonel.

Three F-2 agents, Sergeant M.M., the informant, and I

made up the patrol, which left Armenia in search of the
bandolero. We traveled by car to a point about nine miles
short of Victoria on the highway that goes to Holguín. After
having traveled for nine hours—it was now almost six o'clock
Friday morning—we holed up in a *cafetal*. Half the patrol
slept while the others kept watch and made observations with
field glasses.

At three that afternoon we spotted Puente Roto, in
company with two other *bandoleros*, Piquiña and Sapa. We
might have captured or killed them then if it hadn't been for
the steep terrain and the distance that separated us.

The trio was moving up the mountain road quite a way
above us. To encourage us, the informant advised that we
change our position because he was sure Puente Roto would
come back down the mountain the next day.

Following this change of position our hardships began:
the F-2 agents did not have rations so we others had to share
ours with them, and that night we had nothing at all left to
eat.*

---

*The survival instruction given in the Lancer training prepares the indi-
vidual soldier to survive on a very limited amount of food. On certain
assignments, such as the current one. the unit must rely solely on
rations carried. Canned foods, of course, have great nutritional content,
but, in addition to being heavy, they may spoil quickly and cause severe
illness. Once we were near our objective and practically had Conrado
Salazar and all his gang in our grasp when some damned contaminated
food made me and two other soldiers ill. The latter were suffering such
stomach pains and were groaning so loudly that there was nothing to do
but take them to the military post at Puente Samaria. Thereby we lost
our advantage of surprise, and hence, a marvelous opportunity.

Experience has taught me that for these patrols in the wilds the best
things to carry are *panela* and water. The sugar cake can be scraped and
these scrapings, mixed with powdered milk, can be pressed into pellets,
which are easily carried in pocket or knapsack. With *panela*, water,
sandals, weapon, ammunition, and hand grenades the patrolling soldier
can be considered logistically supplied for a mission lasting up to
seventy-two hours.

As much as possible, he should avoid living off the civilian population;

We kept waiting, the hours passingly slowly and fruit-lessly. At eleven on Saturday morning, however, we sighted the *bandolero*—in the company of the police inspector of that rural area and a judge from a large city, the owner of a nearby hacienda!

The sight of that trio filled us with great indignation. It was impossible to accept this alliance of the criminal with those charged with exercising authority and administering justice. Could my eyes be deceiving me? Definitely not! I was not mistaken. There, in a gross affront to society, were the representative of the government, the magistrate, and the murderer, all three joined in hellish hobnobbery.

Had we arrived at such abysmal immorality?

The inspector, the judge, and the *bandolero* continued along their distant path without our being able to do any-thing except record in our notebooks what our retinas re-ceived, in order to report it to brigade headquarters later. Our waiting resumed. We were in a bamboo thicket, being tor-tured by swarms of mosquitos, unable to move about lest we betray our presence, enduring the torrents of water that fell from the skies and the pangs of hunger.

That same day, Saturday, a worker from the hacienda accidentally stumbled upon us in the bamboo.

"There goes the mission, sergeant," grumbled the F-2 agents. "That guy will give us away."

"Don't sing the blues yet," I answered them as I covered the intruder with my carbine.

"Come here," I ordered the man, who turned out to be a dairy hand. Turning to the informant, I said: "Tie him up with that rope he's carrying for hauling bamboo." When he was tied up, I talked with him.

"Where is Puente Rojo?"

"I don't know. I don't know him."

---

however, when circumstances make it impossible to avoid doing so, he should arrange to pay in advance for food received. In this respect we differ from the *bandolero*, who oppresses the rural people and steals the bread that the honest laborer has provided for his family.

"If you won't talk willingly, you'd better talk unwillingly."

"Look, I'm a family man. My wife is not well," he implored.

"So what's that to me?" I replied coldly.

"Tell me who you people are. Not knowing, I don't dare say anything. If you are the authorities, I've already told you I don't know Puente Roto."

"And what if we're *bandoleros*, companions of Alonso Llanos [Puente Roto]?" I countered.

"Well, in that case I guess we can talk."

"The odds just went against you and in favor of me," I stated. "Look at this military ID. We are army noncoms."

The stranger stood perplexed and finally said:

"I know you're going to kill me. They did this to me before, over at Sevilla, to find out if I was a supporter. Some *bandoleros* strung me up from a rafter and while I was hanging there they asked me about Puente Roto. I swore I didn't know him and they swore they were authorities. But they didn't identify themselves the way you did. Let me loose and we'll talk then. By tomorrow we can trap him."

"Don't turn him loose," cried the informant. "If he goes free he'll finger me and get me killed."

"So you know this man?" I asked the informant.

"All too well. I was the administrator of this hacienda, sergeant, and this traitor was a dairy hand of mine. We knew one another and we helped Puente Roto. There are things that should not be mentioned, but I suppose you will have to know them. . . . On a certain occasion Puente Roto came to my house, pointed his gun at me, and had me tied to a tree all night while he stayed with my wife. I swore revenge and that's why I'm here with you looking for him. The *bandoleros* are cowards; they attack as a gang or they take you by surprise. You could kill me as a collaborator, because many times I sheltered Puente Roto in my house; you see how he repaid me!"

"I promise I'll help you," declared the dairy hand. "This afternoon Puente Roto has to go to the house to get clothes.

If he comes down from the other side, from La Palmera, I'll go to the gate to close it and I'll come tell you."

"How much time do you want to deliver Puente Roto to us?" I demanded.

"You'll have him before tomorrow afternoon."

"I'm going to let you go, but you are not to leave your house, and if that bird gets away from us it'll be because you warned him and I'll settle accounts with you personally."

We turned him loose and instructed him to make sure we were able to see him every hour.

About seven in the evening the man whistled to us from the gate. He said that the *bandolero* had been in the house, that he was half drunk, and that he had left to go to La Palmera.

At ten o'clock we were at La Palmera. But apparently no matter how long we waited or what we did, Puente Roto was not to appear.

For three days we stayed there, nibbling on sugar cane and deceiving our stomachs with dirty water from the brooks. Eventually, however, Sergeant X.X. and I decided to return to Armenia to rest and then take up the mission again with better logistical support.

We were departing frustrated by three days of unproductive work; but that's the way war is, a succession of victories and defeats—up to the final battle. Suddenly the sun broke out, bathing the jagged topography with its morning light. We were resting at a spot covered with trees and, since it was market day, we decided to check the people who were coming to the town nearby.

At about eight o'clock that morning the informant and I were high in a tree when we saw some horses in the patio of a hacienda called Marabú.

"Those are Puente Roto's horses," declared the informant. "He must be there because he doesn't like to walk anywhere." Moments later he stated with emotion: "There he is!"

He handed me the field glasses and I could easily see a man, about twenty-eight years old, dressed in white, with a wide-brimmed, white sombrero, who wore two revolvers, three MK-2 grenades, and a Mexican-style bandoleer.

"They're serving him breakfast," I told our companions, who were waiting impatiently at the foot of the tree.

"Now he's saddling up a chestnut horse. . . . He just put on a poncho to cover his guns and bandoleer. . . . Men, he's mounted and is riding out of the corral."

I scrambled down to the ground, assembled the patrol, and addressed them calmly: "He's on his way."

An F-2 agent, Sergeant X.X., and I ran as fast as we could to a spot beside the dirt road along which Alfonso would have to come.

As he reached the end of the road leading to the Marabú hacienda, he waved to those who were in the house. Just then from a kneeling position behind a thicket I shouted to him: "'Fonso! 'Fonso!"

He turned to look around, surprised that someone should be calling him by name.

"Hands up!" I shouted. But he was not about to give up docilely. He answered with the deadly roar of his revolvers.

A burst of carbine fire hit horse and rider. Puente Roto fell clear and kept firing over the horse, whose body served as a support. He fired with amazing rapidity. He tossed a grenade, but it fell far short of where we were. Realizing he was lost, he tried a trick the *bandoleros* often use in such circumstances: he draped his arms over the horse's body and pretended to be dead.

"Don't go near him, sergeant," I cried anxiously. He's still alive." I circled around behind him and, covering him with my revolver (because I had no more carbine ammunition), I called on him to surrender. But Puente Roto, who had been hoping for an imprudent move on our part in order to kill us, tried to make use of his weapons. I didn't give him time to do so. He threw up his arms one last time as he fell back to the ground—to this earth, which was the grave of more than one hundred and fifty victims of this murderer.

Vain had been the efforts of many patrols and missions, traversing innumerable miles of roads in the Quindío and in

Valle. Puente Roto had even mocked the Colombia Battalion, thanks to the protective silence of the civilian population, which, through fear of reprisals, did not dare to denounce him.

On a mule from the hacienda, we transported the body while we, on horseback, rode toward the police station at San José. An F-2 agent and I rode on ahead with the intention of informing the police and arranging for the loan of some vehicles. Some citizens, on seeing us approach, armed and so frightful in appearance, and thinking we must be *bandoleros*, turned their cars around and drove full speed to warn the police.

When we arrived at San José the police had set up an ambush for us. We threw our arms to the ground. I got down from my horse, raised my hands, and asked, "Who's in charge here?"

A sergeant walked forward, eyeing us with distrust.

"I am Sergeant 2nd Buitrago of the Army," I said. "We've just killed Puente Roto."

"Yeah? And what else is new?"

He was convinced we were *bandoleros* and that we had come to set up some kind of trap.

We were held in jail incommunicado. Showing our ID cards was to no avail. Fortunately the rest of the patrol soon appeared with the body.

The joy of the police and the townspeople was immense. They made our week's hunger disappear with their gifts; the good people never stopped thanking God for the fortunate event. Once more they would be able to work their fields, harvest the coffee, carry the fruits of their labors to market, go to church, and go to sleep without the fear of attack, arson, and murder.

We were taken in a police car to Cartago, and from there we continued to Armenia.

The mortal remains of Alfonso Llanos, a native of Calarcá, alias Puente Roto, now beginning to putrify, lay in the patio of brigade headquarters; beside the body were lined up the

two hand grenades, the two revolvers, a set of handcuffs, and
the bandoleer.

General S.S., who was making an inspection trip, compli-
mented us on the outcome of the mission. Colonel V.V. did
so, too.

51 · Those Blessed Blades

Thus, one reaches the stars.

Our country owes much to its military pilots, especially its
helicopter pilots. May God and the government be mindful of
them.

Before the 8th Brigade received them, I had never flown
in an Iroquois or in a Kaman. I was acquainted with small
helicopters and considered them the best means of transportation. The helicopter, with its ability to take off from
any spot without a runway, to fly like any airplane, and to
land on a rooftop or any place a few yards square, meets the
most stringent requirements.

This apparatus, which flies by means of the rotation of
horizontal blades, would seem to have been invented precisely for participation in the war against the *bandoleros*. Its
use in reconnoitering, supply, evacuation, etc., is recom-
mended by several years' experience. Without it, dozens of
gravely wounded, of whom the author of this book has been
one, would have perished. Without it, many operations could
never have been undertaken or would have failed.

There is nothing like the helicopter for psychological warfare, and on this topic I should like to describe something
that happened to me. Captain M.M., Brigade B-5, and I were
dropping propaganda leaflets over the territory controlled by
Gata and Conrado Salazar.

From the air, I recognized the regions that we had
covered in patrols—the streams, the hills, the meadows, the

haciendas. We had been flying for about half an hour without incident and had dropped a good number of leaflets when the Devil, who cannot remain silent, stucks his claws into our delicate machinery. Although not well versed in motors, we were nevertheless able to perceive strange noises. The captain and I paled and looked at each other, and then we looked to the pilot for some sign that would confirm our uneasiness. But the lieutenant operated the controls calmly, as if nothing were wrong—not because he did not know what was happening but in order to reassure us. A few minutes later the Hiller craft went into a free fall and hit the ground. The lieutenant, with unusual coolheadedness, had accomplished a maneuver known as autorotation, and had softened our crash against a clump of bamboo.

It was rather like being born again, we noted, as we palpably confirmed to ourselves that we had intact heads, bodies, and limbs.

Next, the lieutenant checked over the helicopter and found it to be all right; fortunately, nothing appeared to have been broken in the crash.

Quickly we evaluated the situation.

"Captain, we're in Gata's territory."

"If we abandon the machine the *bandoleros* will burn it," the captain observed. Our fright was considerable and not without good cuase.

"If the *bandoleros* saw our spectacular descent they must be on their way here, and there's nothing we can do about it," I declared.

We had only two revolvers and two hand grenades among us, while the *bandoleros* would be able to attack us from a distance with the fire of their automatic weapons.

"Captain, may I suggest that you and the pilot go to get help? Or if you wish, I will go."

"I'm not leaving the helicopter," declared the lieutenant. "This is my place, and I'll die here."

The situation was precarious, because if we took the road to Quimbaya, we would probably run into Joselito's men; if we went toward Alcalá, Conrado Salazar and Hiena would destroy us; if we tried to get to Montenegro, worst of all, there were the marauders Gata and Llanero.

In the area where we were, ordinarily three *cuadrillas* operated. Our salvation was in the heavens and to the skies we turned our glances. The lieutenant, after examing the helicopter again, said:

"Dirty gasoline. I'm going to try to start it." It started.

"I'll try to get the bird up again," said the pilot. "You can decide whether you want to climb in. We may bump again."

"I'm not even thinking about getting back in that thing," said the captain.

"Captain," I suggested, "it's better to risk it. If we're supposed to die, we'll die. It's better for us to die all of a sudden than to be cut into little pieces by the machetes of Conrado or Gata."

"You're right," the captain agreed.

"Don't be so pessimistic," said the lieutenant. "I was just talking; everything's fixed."

And once again we were in the air, though quite worried about a possible reoccurrence of the mechanical failure. Old Nick had lots of tricks that day, and he apparently had no other diversion than our craft because five minutes after the second lift-off, the blasted motor began to cough. Let the bravest of men tell me there was no reason to have goose bumps.

During those critical moments we were all ears listening to the motor, and all eyes watching the reactions of the lieutenant. As before, he betrayed no emotion. Suddenly the motor quit and captain, pilot, and sergeant plummeted toward the earth. With all serenity the pilot executed the appropriate maneuvers and saved us from certain death and the craft from complete destruction.

This time we had landed, fortunately, not far from the military post at Montenegro.

Permit me to recount something similar that happened, so I've been told, around 1952 in the *llanos* of Casanare. The

undeclared civil war was at its height in our country. Lieu-
tentant-Colonel P.P., commander of the Maza Cavalry Group,
was making a flight over the eastern cordillera to reach
Bogotá, but the weather turned bad and the plane had to
turn back toward Arauca. At five-thirty in the afternoon the
motor failed and the pilot had to make an emergency landing
in a region infested with guerrilla units. The pilot managed to
radio the tower at Apiay the coordinates of their position.
The compassionate darkness of night spread its protective
mantle over passengers and crew, who, lacking arms and
trusting to luck, took refuge in the thickets of the wilds. With
the dawn of the next day a large number of *bandoleros* began
to move in on the plane in response to a bugle call. They
were getting ready to burn the plane and to search the environs for its occupants when planes of the FAC (Colombian
Air Force) appeared in the sky. Their machine-gun fire dispersed the *bandoleros* and made it possible for a DC-3 to land
with mechanics and troops. A short time later the planes returned to Apiay with no loss of personnel, but with their
wings full of bullet holes.

Not attempting to follow any particular chronological
order, I include here the story of my first flight in a helicopter and how airsick I was. It was in an Iroquois and we
were flying along at an altitude of several hundred feet when
a wave of nausea swept over me and I had to vomit. So that
the pilot and especially Major L.L. would not be aware of my
condition, I used the only thing available—my service cap.
When we arrived at the military post of Puente Samaria, the
major, seeing me bareheaded, snapped:
"Sergeant Buitrago, put on your cap!"
I was not exactly in a position to obey the order, so I
hesitated, which caused the officer to dress me down.
The military being the military, I obeyed the order and
put on my cap, whereupon its contents began to slide over
my forehead, around my ears, and down the back of my
neck. Amidst the laughter of the spectators, especially the
soldiers, I was obliged to withdraw as rapidly as possible to a
nearby kitchen to wash myself.

More recent is what happened at Caicedonia. One afternoon, during a Civic Action demonstration or something of
the sort, a Hiller helicopter brushed a power line and crashed.
Because it had been flying at a low altitude there were no
injuries to personnel, but the ship was damaged. Subsequently it was towed to Armenia on a trailer from the Cis-
neros Battalion. The entire operation, being such an unusual
occurrence, caused great excitement among the civilian and
military populace.

In another incident, the *bandolero* Sangrenegra kidnapped a wealthy doctor and hacienda owner from Pereira
and demanded from the relatives fifty thousand pesos as ransom. Taking advantage of his guard's inattention, the kidnapped man hit the guard in the head with a bench and fled,
hoping to escape. The *bandoleros*, however, overtook him in
a meadow and shot him down with a volley.

To recover the body it was necessary to transport troops
by helicopter to the Guatemala hacienda, owned by the
deceased, at the border of Caldas and Tolima. This task was
carried out by Captain D.D.'s flying a Kaman under conditions
of virtually zero visibility, he landed, as they say, by the seat
of his pants. The troops and the *bandoleros* sustained a prolonged fire fight, which resulted in one sergeant 2nd class
wounded and two *bandoleros* dead.

I went with Major L.L. on the third helicopter flight, but
the *bandoleros* were already in flight.

I could go on describing many more truly notable acts
performed by our brave military pilots in the service of public order.

As for my personal recollection, I can say I have unforgettable memories of the FAC, and especially of its helicopter pilots, and their important collaboration with the 8th
Brigade and the missions we had to undertake. Allow me to
finish this chapter by paying homage to the memory of the
officer, whose name I do not now recall, who perished, the

victim of the *cuadrilla* of Tirofijo.† This pilot, after conquering the massif of the central cordillera, landed in Tolima to try to rescue an Avianca pilot.

Someday someone will write in full detail the history of the role of the "Knights of the Air" in the struggle against *la violencia*. Their deeds in the *llanos* of Casanere between 1949 and 1953, for example, would supply material for many books.

Until some future pen will preserve these outstanding acts of our military history, I shall be content for the moment by publicly expressing my admiration for the FAC with these words:

"Blessed blades!"

52 · Boyeyo

If you wish peace, prepare for war.

The San Mateo Battalion requested my services and, the commander of the 8th Brigade being willing, I reported in Pereira, accompanied by two noncoms with whom I worked well.

Our mission, an important one, was to capture the *bandolero* known as Boyeyo, the scourge of western Caldas, who massacred rural folk and then took refuge in Sultana in Valle. Among his numerous crimes I recall specifically the assassination of the judge of Apía, whom he killed because the judge was proceeding with an investigation, and the kidnapping of Don Fulgencio Jiménez, of Pereira, from whom he received

---

† "Tirofijo" (Sureshot) is Manuel Marulanda Vélez, leader of the Fuerzas Armadas Revolucionarias de Colombia (FARC), a procommunist coalition of guerrilla and bandit gangs in Tolima. He is the only *bandolero* in the *violencia* to hold a position on the Central Committee of the Colombian Communist Party.

as ransom the trifling sum of six hundred thousand pesos. The major, two corporals, the informant, and I reached Cali the next day. The major and the two corporals reported to the 3rd Brigade, while the informant and I went to reconnoiter the part of town frequented by *bandoleros*.

Shortly thereafter I entered a bar and asked for a carbonated drink. I slowly sipped my drink, observing the scene, catching words, and finally I leaned over to the barman and said in a low voice:

"Tell me, where can I find Boyeyo? I've got a letter of reference from a man in Viterbo. I'm the leader of the rest of Pote's *cuadrilla*. Pote is presently under arrest in Bogotá."

The bartender did not appear suspicious and replied amiably: "Boyeyo doesn't hang around much; he's planning a kidnapping." When the clock said five in the afternoon and the potential kidnapper still had not appeared, I departed, leaving a message that a member of Pote's *cuadrilla* needed Boyeyo to carry out an assignment in Cali.

I hastened to the brigade headquarters and gave this information to Major X. I asked the assistance of the two noncoms, whom I then left in the park, to which I planned to lead the *bandolero* by some ruse. At nine that evening I was ushered into a house where the notorious Boyeyo was seated along with two other men.

"Welcome, friend. They've told me about you." He gave me his hand. "Your chief is well known; you should be very proud to belong to Pote's band. He is famous, you might say, for his banking interests."

"This time I'm not here on a bank robbery," I replied. "I'm here to arrange a kidnapping."

"You got here just in time," stated Boyeyo, "and you're going to get to take part in a very big kidnapping that I've already got worked out. We are going to demand a million, not a cent less."

We dined sumptuously and, dinner over, I suggested to them that we take a walk through the park. But my plans were thwarted because this fellow, either through suspicion or because he was too tired, decreed that we all would go to bed early right there.

I would have to devise some other way to maneuver him into a sure trap. Also I wanted to discover as many of his hirelings and collaborators as I could.

The next day this fine gentleman took me downtown for breakfast and then back to his house; he was very friendly toward me and very solicitous.

"What weapons do you have?"

"Just a revolver," I answered.

"Let me see it; let's have a look."

"Sure, Boyeyo."

I unloaded it and handed it to him. Whereupon this tricky fellow looked at the 8.5 for a moment then suddenly pointed it at me and barked:

"What would you do if I decided to hand you over to the police?"

"I wouldn't do anything Boyeyo," I said, and then with my fast draw I had him covered with the other revolver I carried.

"Monito, that was just a joke," he stammered, frightened.

"You'd better be careful who you joke with; it won't be with me."

"You're pretty sharp," growled Boyeyo. "And what a fast draw! Pal, I just did that to scare you. How could you imagine I'd do such a thing? You can be very helpful to me. I can see that the things you know are very valuable."

He handed me back the revolver. I reloaded it and put it back in its holster.

"All right," I told him. "It's late and I'm going to Palmira to locate me a back-up man and to pick up a couple of sub-machine guns."

"Of course," said Boycyo. "Those guns will come in very handy!"

"I'm off. Tomorrow at nine we'll meet . . . wherever you say."

We agreed to meet in the park and Boyeyo was to bring with him his two friends so my new man, a touchy, suspicious sort, could meet them all.

"I've got a light truck. If you want to you can use it," offered Boyeyo.

"Thanks, but I have one in Palmira. It's a white one, easy to spot. When you see it in the park you'll know I'm there."

Major C.C. had become exceedingly concerned when I failed to return to brigade headquarters the night before. After I had described the events that had taken place, the major and I mapped out the next stage of the operation. The two corporals, to be stationed strategically in the park, would play an important part.

Nine o'clock in the morning in the city of Cali. The smell of spring, with sunlight streaming down on streets and avenues.

Right on time, Boyeyo appeared with his two companions. He whistled. I did not show that I had heard but sought instead to verify the presence of the two noncoms. They were at their posts. I stopped the vehicle and Boyeyo and one of his companions approached and began a conversation. The dialogue was just chitchat and it dragged on for fifteen minutes, which for me seemed to be fifteen centuries of waiting.

I had to capture them, but I was not able to use my revolvers in that position.

"Get out and come on over to my truck," Boyeyo said suddenly.

He could not have given me a better invitation. On opening the door, I covered them with my guns and shouted: "You're under arrest!"

His companion tried to pull out his weapon but I warned them:

"If you value your lives, don't make a move."

One corporal disarmed them while the other captured the third man, who was trying to run away.

At this moment Major C.C. and a captain from the garrison arrived. The trio of *bandoleros* went to the 3rd Brigade guardhouse.

That same day we took the three prisoners to Pereira. Since Boyeyo, among other crimes, was charged with the murder of a judge, we were instructed to make him available for questioning by the public prosecutor.

We were traveling to Apía in my truck, escorted by a guard traveling in a military station wagon. Boyeyo, who was with me, offered me a hundred thousand pesos in exchange for his freedom. This was certainly a tempting proposition for a noncom who scarecly makes enough to live on day by day. However, there are things more valuable than money—conscience and professional honor.

I heard an explosion and thought it was a shot, but a soldier saw that a tire had blown out. We had stopped and were getting ready to change the tire. Boyeyo, taking advantage of the situation, quick as a wink opened the door and was running for the *cafetal.*

"Halt! Halt! Halt!" the two corporals shouted. Boyeyo ran all the faster.

I aimed my gun and fired over the top of the vehicle. Despite the distance, Boyeyo was hit in the head and fell dead.

Thus ended the life of one of the most audacious *bandoleros* of Caldas.

53 · New Year's Eve

New year, new life!

The military post at Pueblo Rico had in custody a lad, perhaps sixteen years old, who had been caught carrying a letter from the *bandolero* Picardías to his father, in Cali.

The most interesting thing about the letter, which included a snapshot and two hundred pesos in bills, was the invitation the aforementioned *bandolero* extended to his progenitor to join him at a *finca* in the settlement of Gigante, in Montenegro, to celebrate Christmas Eve with wild boar and custard. The letter added that if they could not arrange the big feed on the 24th of December, they would do so for New Year's.

Captain X, from the coast and a man of much common

sense, ordered one of the noncoms to assume the role of the messenger and to deliver the letter in Cali. (The original messenger remained in custody.)

While the corporal was successfully carrying out this mission, having joined the family circle of Picardías' kin, another noncom and I were on our way to the *finca*. We had hopes of bushwhacking the genial host, Picardías, and perhaps also Gata, Grillo, Avispa, and Pastillas.

In that low-lying region we experienced a suffocating heat, to which were added the attacks of swarms of flies, that made mincemeat of our necks, faces, hands, and fingers, and the punishment of rain that descended from the heavens in torrents, as if the Flood were about to be repeated. So there we sat, out in the weather, stoically enduring the showers. When it would clear off and the sun appeared, our clothes, clinging to our skin, gave off steam as they slowly dried. In the afternoon, before the arrival of swarms of the malaria-bearing anopheles, a diminutive insect attacked our miserable bodies—the *jejen*, the biting midge or sandfly. As the rhyme goes:

> When the sandfly's bite you do perceive
> Then you know it's time for you to leave.

Conditions only worsened at night and the cold, combining with the night dew, made our physical misery complete. It seemed the elements were allies of the *bandoleros.*

We did not want to leave our position, so when the call of nature became absolutely unbearable we dug shallow holes in the earth and after relieving ourselves filled the holes to be sure there would be no odor to betray our presence to the nearby house. We reminded ourselves of cats.

Such personal and imtimate details—not repugnant but rather, human—merit being known as a part of guerrilla life.

Waiting and more waiting—eyes scanning the horizon, the paths, the surrounding vegetation. Have patience, we kept saying to ourselves. Soon the guests will arrive for the Christmas feast and our aches and pains will be rewarded by their capture.

Christmas Eve; oh, peaceful night!
Stars and moon shed loving light.

Christmas Eve. Happiness in the cities; joy in the countryside; a myriad of colorful lights in the towns; records that pour out joyous melodies, and fireworks that deafen the bystanders. In the Quindío, despite all its agony, its tragedy, despite Conrado and his *cuadrilla*, one hears words of hope in the songs, peaceful melodies from the guitars, joy and exhilaration from the tiples—all these bless the coming of the Lord. At that time, as at no other, one perceives the full religious significance of the joys of the novena of the Christ Child:

Come to our spirits!
Come, do not delay!

There was a festive air about this house in the country. Bottles released provocative aromas; rockets soared toward the clouds; pigs squealed, feet tied together, awaiting the sacrifice that would convert their bodies into cracklings and their insides into succulent pudding. The pots were aboil with the traditional custard, and the hot, honey-glazed buns gave off their appealing smell.

From our hiding place amid the branches and the shadows we observed this extraordinary activity. And to think that at that moment, back at the brigade, our comrades in arms would be gathered around the Christmas tree; in the noncoms' club there would be dancing, and presents; something special to drink and the special foods would impart a warmth and happiness to the celebration of the memorial night. Our wives, distressed by our absence, would say a prayer beside the creche, mercifully deceiving the children with the promise we would return at any moment.

All that we got for Christmas were sleepiness, fatigue, and hunger. How miserable we were. Midnight! Merry Christmas, Baby Jesus!

And the *bandoleros* never came. What a fiasco!

We waited, nevertheless, until the 27th, at which time we

decided to return to headquarters. However, since the intercepted letter had made provision for a reunion for New Year's, we rested a few hours in Armenia, and then we returned to our observation post.

It rained continuously. My companion, Sergeant 1st E.E., in order to cheer us up, made an "old" saying: "I won't complain about the rain, Lord—it could be stones, or it could be bullets."

On passing near houses we could hear phonographs and radios repeating endlessly the song:

> New Year's Eve, the night is so clear;
> Heart and soul, I come to you, dear.
> It's with you I want to spend New Year.

Drinking, dancing, music, a midnight supper—this is the summary of the feast of St. Silvester in the countryside of Caldas.

And we, the sentinels of law and order, kept our vigil in the brush. When the fireworks proclaimed the region's jubilation over the arrival of the new year, we crossed ourselves slowly and thought of our families. In place of our children's heads, we caressed the weapons that the republic had trusted to our undeserving hands.

"Suffer and don't cry—just like the song says," advised the sergeant.

Neither Gata nor his cohorts came to the *finca*.

"What the hell," we philosophized. "Maybe next time."

The second day of the new year we spent in Armenia. The failure of our extended mission had not broken our spirit.

54 · An Encounter with Gata

*The important thing is not that the one in front is
running, but that the one behind does not tire.*

A *bandolero* had been captured in Alcalá, and the civil and
military authorities thought it might be Gata.

A series of interrogations did not clarify matters. The suspect was taken to Pereira and questioned again, but with no
better results. He was then brought to the headquarters of
the 8th Brigade. Since I had been with Gata in Conrado
Salazar's *cuadrilla*, I was able to clear up one point:

"He doesn't look a bit like Gata."

Our very careful questioning clarified things: this was
Avispa, Gata's lieutenant.

"If you won't kill me and will give me some money, I'll
deliver to you the man you're looking for," said Avispa.

"We won't kill you because that is not our responsibility;
and we will pay you for each rifle or carbine recovered and
for each *bandolero* captured."

Four noncoms of the Mobile Group of the brigade, four
noncoms from the cavalry troop, and the informant comprised the unit that was to operate under my command. We
tested our weapons.*

We traveled by night, in a weapons carrier, to the military
post at Riberalta, where we left the vehicle and requested a
noncom who knew the region to accompany us.

---

*Before going out on a mission it is indispensible to test the weapons,
to verify the proper functioning of the mechanism, to adjust the gas
ports, etc. From each lot of hand grenades, two or three should be
selected at random and detonated to check their functioning and their
effect. The automatic rifle is too heavy. Whenever possible, each patrol
member should carry two firearms—one of long-range capability and
the other for personal defense. I patrolled with a carbine, a pistol or
revolver, two hand grenades, and a machete. In the shoot-out with
Puente Roto, when I ran out of carbine ammunition, I used my
revolver.

We continued cross-country on foot, following the directions of Avispa, now our voluntary informant. We skirted around the town of San Isidro and at five in the morning we reached our first objective. We wore the *ruana* and sombrero, typical dress of the region, but beneath the *ruana* we wore our military uniforms.

From five until eleven in the morning we watched a house where Gata had a girl friend. "He's not there," Avispa said. "He would have come out by now."

We resumed our climb along the steep slopes, stopping to observe the few houses we passed.

Suddenly the sound of music reached our ears. It was a phonograph and after listening a few minutes Avispa said he could tell who was there by the records being played.

"That one is so-and-so's favorite . . . and that is so-and-so's record. Look," he said, pointing out a house some two hundred yards distant. "There is where all of them are."

We could see several men grouped around a patio. As a security measure while traveling I had divided the patrol. I now assembled the men and encouraged them as I pointed out the *bandoleros*. One of the noncoms and the informant thought we would be able to attack at dawn with the best chance of success.

"We have to take the house this afternoon," I replied. "At dawn they might slip by us."

I conscientiously evaluated the situation, made my decision and issued the order:

"Corporal A., take half the men and close off the uphill side of the house, starting there at the century plants. I'll take the other men and close off the downhill side. Set your watches; it's exactly one thirty. At three every man will be at the position assigned. I'll give the signal to start firing."

It took us almost an hour and a half to cover less than two hundred yards, creeping and crawling so as not to be seen by the enemy. There was a lookout on the patio who scanned the environs with field glasses.

We could hear quite clearly the battery-operated record player as it blared out a Mexican tune extolling the guerrilla life, a tune very popular, to be sure, in the *cantinas* and cafés of the Quindío.

"Four bullets whined . . .," went the song.

For several months we had been pursuing Gata without success, across brook and forest, through hamlet and *cafetal*. A few weeks before, this *bandolero*, whose name was Jesús Eliécer Sepúlveda Estrada, had kidnapped a woman from Quimbaya, the owner of a hacienda, and had received seventy thousand pesos ransom. A short time before that he had kidnapped a wealthy hacienda owner from Montenegro and ransomed him for two hundred thousand pesos. The story was that the *bandolero* spent seventy thousand of this ransom in the purchase of ten submachine guns, and he gave the money to a lieutenant of his, called Mocho.

Now we were so close to Sepúlveda we could hear him speaking. His bright eyes, which flashed diabolically when he used a machete on some unfortunate farmer or rifled a victim's body, were less than fifty yards from us.

Would this mission fail? Would all our efforts be in vain? No!

Everything was just about ready and I was about to give the signal. I was crossing a brook when the enemy opened fire. They had seen us! Gata and two others made a break down the slope.

After fifteen minutes of firing he was dead.

The firing pin broke in the M-1 of the corporal who was with me, and I was out of ammunition. The fire fight was heavy above, below, and on both sides of the house.

With a superrapid movement I hurled myself on the body of Gata, seized his cartridge belt and was supplied with ammunition again. His carbine was just like mine.

I took over and began firing again.

For forty-five minutes the intense firing from both sides continued. But success was with us because we properly applied the principles of surprise and maneuver.

The outcome of the action: eight *bandoleros* dead; four San Cristóbal carbines reovered, plus two .30 calibre rifles, a Colt .45, a revolver, and several MK-2 hand grenades.

Our troops fought fearlessly, with discipline and precision, as befits experienced veterans of guerrilla warfare. We
suffered not a single casualty and no loss of weapons or
equipment.

After retracing our route of the previous night, we
reached San Isidro at seven in the evening. There vehicles of
the Vencedores Battalion picked up our patrol and the bodies
of the *bandoleros.*

55 · How to Do Away with the *Cuadrillas*

The first thing to do is start.

How easy it is for an aficionado of bullfighting, sitting com-
fortably in the stands, to be critical of a pass by El Cordobés.
How easy it is to boo when a soccer player fails to make a
goal, while one sits there smoking or eating or even drinking
in the box seats of the stadium. But how different it is to feel
oneself completely alone in the arena, with no weapon but a
cape, facing half a ton of Mondoñedo bull that is charging.
And how one appreciates the plays in their true perspective
when one dons the soccer team's jersey.

We can make the same observations about certain operations in the program to restore law and order in Colombia. It
would seem to be a fairly easy matter to follow an informant
thirty miles or more in search of the *bandoleros'* hideout, to
locate them, to fight them, to capture them or kill them—
wouldn't it?

But how many missions fail because the *bandoleros,*
knowing the terrain or warned beforehand by civilians, flee
to distant haunts! How much honest blood has moistened
our earth in the effort to destroy the *bandoleros!*

We noted in a previous chapter that *la violencia* is the

worst scourge that can afflect a country. As I transmit my memoirs to my Remington, the newspapers of La Paz and Lima speak of centers of guerrilla activity just two hundred miles from Lima; they speak of subversive activities on the frontier between Brazil and Bolivia; they speak of sabotage and terrorism carried out by the Venezuelan Fuerzas Armadas de Liberation Nacional.

As I leaf through the book of Colombian martyrs of the last fifteen years, I hope our sister nations will not have to deal with situations as difficult as those that confronted us in Colombia.

Our struggle was a hard one. Thousands of victims were slain on the byroads and in the settlements. But the flag of Colombia, created under the guardianship of the greatest of the Americans, Simón Bolívar, continues to display its colors on the peaks of the Andes and in the burning valleys. This flag, proclaiming our sovereignty, will never be struck so long as the great majority of Colombians preserve their heritage.

Today, having overcome in a painful campaign, noncoms, soldiers, and agents have gained an experience that enables them to face the most adverse circumstances.

So, thanks to the vigilance of the authorities, to the energy and determination of the armed forces, and the cooperation of the citizenry, our institutions, our beliefs, and our customs have been preserved.

Peace has returned to the cities and to the countryside; the few trouble spots to be found here and there in the expanse of our country are but the last redoubts of those bad citizens who one day tried to betray their country.

Puente Roto, as ferocious as Sangrenegra or Chispas, fell with no intention of surrendering, just as another notorious *bandolero* did not intend to surrender in the country's capital.

Puente Roto lay six feet under ground but his close collaborators, "armed to the teeth"—to use a very Colombian metaphor—remained as a potential threat to the fertile region of the Quindío.

Thanks to the cooperation that the inhabitants of the

region began to manifest toward the army, a month after the action against Alfonso Llanos two more *bandoleros*, Piquiña and Sapa, fell to the fire of our rifles. We recovered two Madsen submachine guns, MK-2 grenades, revolvers, and ammunition.

Other *bandoleros*, frightened, left the region.

The refugees began to return to their abandoned *fincas*. Entire families, who had been suffering from hunger in the cities to which they had fled to escape the crimes of the *bandoleros*, returned to their land. Children romped again in the yards, as a sign of the better days to come.

Now the owners of *fincas* come to brigade headquarters to ask for instructions, and now owners and workers alike denounce the criminals. The army has won the most important battle—it has won the confidence of the people.

Let us remember: "A revolutionary war needs the unconditional support of the civilian population if it is to be initiated and to prosper." "There is a struggle between the revolutionaries, who seek to attract the populace and make them participants in the subversion, and the forces of order, who try to hinder or to neutralize those efforts."

It is the responsibility of the military forces and the police to counteract the revolutionary action by various means: (a) by directing the *autodefensa*, or defense of the populace through its own resources, and (b) by seeking the support of the people for the forces of order and the legitimate government. This is effected through irreproachable conduct, effective action against the *bandoleros*, and through the Acción Cívica Militar (the Civil-Military Action program).

Public support having been won by the forces of order, the revolution was lost.

56 · The End of Mono Orozco

You will be measured with your own yardstick.

On the ninth day of February in that year of grace 1965, a shipment of money from the Commercial Bank of Armenia was being sent to the branch in Calarcá. Knowledgeable robbers took from the messengers the attractive sum of four hundred and six thousand pesos in currency. This crime was capped by the killing of the police guard, José Gilberto Quiroga Fandiño.

The holdup men were very well informed as to the route of the shipment. They had stationed a light truck down the block from the bank, and, when the bank messengers got into their car and drove away, the robbers pulled out also but, being down the block, they preceded the bank car. At a stop sign the truck stopped, the bank car stopped immediately behind it, and a third car pulled up just in back of the bank car. Thus the bank car could move neither forward nor backward.

Several bandits dashed from the car in the rear. One of them carried a concealed Madsen submachine gun, and when he reached the policeman escorting the shipment, he fired twenty-five rounds into the car, and the guardian of law and order, Quiroga, fell, riddled with bullets, on the front seat of the car. Not content with carrying off the money, they took Quiroga's San Cristóbal carbine before they swiftly departed. One more victim of the madness of these lowlifes, who stop at nothing in carrying out their crimes and thereby bring grief to families whose only sources of support are the inadequate salaries of the sacrificing policemen.

The DAS and F-2 agents devoted a month and a half to fruitless investigations. It had been learned, however, that the leader of the robbers was Guillermo Orozco, alias Mono.

Information reached the 8th Brigade headquarters concerning the presence at a certain house in Armenia of some suspicious-looking men who came and went at all hours of the night. We immediately put the house under surveillance, but without any satisfactory results. However, we did succeed in striking up an acquaintance with a young man who knew the occupants of the house. We said to him:

"Since they're not suspicious of you, lad, find out for us if they are *bandoleros*. Get to know everyone who comes there and bring us information."

The youth played his part extremely well. It is fitting that we recognize his contributions, for to his zeal we owed the favorable developments that took place.

"The ones who are there," he said when he reported to us later, "are the ones who held up the Commercial Bank car. But there are only two of them."

"Is Guillermo Orozco there?"

"No, sergeant. He's not one of them."

Since the interests of society are best served by arresting the principals in a crime, we returned to brigade headquarters to wait for a better opportunity.

I gave the lad these instructions:

"Tomorrow go back to the house, and if those men are there tell them Grillo Marín has talked to you and he wants you to buy the carbine they have."

The next day, the lad entered the house. We were a prudent distance away and in a state of readiness. About half an hour later he emerged and came to us.

"They're there. They got the carbine out and showed it to me. I just told them I was going out to bring the man who wants to buy it."

"Sergeant," I said, "I'm going to be the buyer. You be my buddy." We went in. Two men seated on the bed greeted us.

"You the one that would like to buy a carbine?" one said.

"Why do you need it?" Guillermo Orozco asked me.

"I'm going to be commander of what's left of Gata's *cuadrilla*," I replied. "I plan to operate right around Montenegro."

"We're going to kidnap a man in Calarcá," stated Mono.

"After we finish that job, I'll sell you the carbine."

"Show me the gun; let me see it. If it works all right I'll forget about another one I've been thinking about buying and wait until you finish what you're going to do."

They handed the carbine over to me with a magazine, but at that moment a third man, who had been listening in the next room, either because he recognized us as law men or simply because he was suspicious, burst into the room, firing his revolver.

A woman present, who had nothing to do with the whole thing, was slain by the bullets of the *bandolero*. Orozco and his companion seized their revolvers, but in vain, because our bullets felled them in seconds.

It had been our intent to capture them alive and bring them to the authorities so they could tell where the money was. But circumstances forced us to fire in order to save our lives.

We handed over to our superiors the carbine stolen from the policeman the day of the holdup, three revolvers, and a good supply of ammunition.

Up to the time of writing this chapter, no one knows where the four hundred and six thousand pesos are hidden. This is quite a sum! In order to amass that amount, a non-com, saving a hundred pesos a month, would have to live to the age of a Biblical patriarch—three hundred and thirty-eight years.

57 · Man Overboard!

Sailors of Colombia, good wind and a good sea!

Not all in war is bullets, nor are all minutes filled with anguish and pain; between one firefight and the next there are moments of recreation and incidents that, by their innocent humor, lessen the tension of life in the service. This story has to do with Quindío region, which was visited in 1963 by the Quinto Curso de Estado Mayor* Especial, of our Escuela Superior de Guerra.†

Colonels A.A. and V.V., Lieutenant-Colonels O.L. and K.K., and naval Captain L.L. were traveling toward Barcelona, Caldas, in an olive-drab weapons carrier bearing military plates.

A few days earlier government forces had killed the *bandolero* Chispas, the author of at least four hundred murders.

It was the middle of the rainy season, and muddy water poured along creek beds in search of rivers that had already overflowed their banks and inundated the bordering regions, causing great damage to inhabitants, livestock, and planted fields.

The vehicle, an open weapons carrier, driven by a reservist of proven experience, was proceeding along a country road that was about as bumpy as a railroad track. At a low spot, the water covered a good stretch of the road, but the driver, a veteran of many rainy seasons, sailed right through the pond with the dexterity of our sailors as they sail through Bocas de Ceniza.

---

*The General Staff of the Army of Liberation was created through a decree of September 24, 1817, in Angostura. The functions and responsibilities of the General Staff were those contained in the *Manual of the Adjutants and Subordinates of the Division General Staff* by Paul Thiebault, which was translated from French by Captain Liborio Mejia. The General Staff of the Liberator functioned from that time on in five sections: Organization of Troops, Administration, Pay and Disbursements, Intelligence, Topography, and Cartography. (General Cortes Vargas)

†The 5th Special Command and General Staff Course at the Superior War School was one of a series of crash courses for staff officers from all the Colombian armed forces. The intensified military-schooling effort was aimed at teaching the field commander and his staff officers about the relationship between socioeconomic problems and military operations in the backlands.

By the time of their return trip from Barcelona, however, the waters had risen several inches, and when the driver once again sailed into the pond the vehicle and its valuable cargo almost capsized, heeling to starboard. The naval officer managed to jump clear and as he did someone shouted, "Man overboard!" If the pond had not been shallow and if the water had not slowed them down, those lieutenant-colonels would not be colonels today, the colonels would not be progressing toward promotion to general, and Captain L.L. would not be in Lima as naval attaché.

Following the old homeopathic maxim, *similia similibus curantur*, at the officers club in Pereira the "shipwrecked" officers were greeted in an appropriate and elegant reception, where they were served whiskey and aged Caldas rum and, of course, water!

Since we are speaking of the navy, it is fitting that mention be made (even if briefly) of the contribution of the members of the Colombian navy to the reestablishment of peace.

In the Quindío, for example, a number of petty officers and specialists served brilliantly as military mayors and worked efficiently in the offices of the general staff of the 8th Brigade. Those of us who served with such distinguished professionals can testify to their capacity for work and, above all, to their spirit of comraderie.

Let us remember, the sailor is to the sea what the infantryman is to the land and the pilot to the air. It is for this reason that the participation of our companions from the navy in the service of public order in the mountains of the Quindío and Tolima is so praiseworthy.

In 1956, the Antares Company (Marines) had the task of pacifying the headwaters of the Cucuana River, the districts of San Francisco and Florida, and the town of Roncesvalles. There our marines received their baptism of fire in the cause of social tranquility.

Going further back in time, to 1952, we see them gliding along the rivers of the departments of Meta, Casanare and Arauca, under the burning sun or on stormy nights, guiding their *lanchas* in search of the enemy, or carrying clothing, food, and medicine to the forsaken populace.

Unfortunately, the particular purpose of this book does not allow me to expand on the role of the navy in the pacification of San Juan de Urabá, Arboletas, Necoclí, Turbo, Acandí, etc.

Let me be content with the affirmation that on salt water or fresh, afloat or ashore, our sailors have been ready to sacrifice themselves for Colombia.

58 · The Cross of Boyacá

Sow, in order to reap.

When they ordered me to go to Bogotá to receive the Cross of Boyacá I thought I was dreaming. The national government wished to recognize my modest services.

It is true—and I do not deny it—that many times during the long vigils of patrolling near the enemy, I had thought of winning that decoration, as the honored complement to the medals that I had already received for services on behalf of public order and for having been wounded in action. I aspired to these loftier heights, and I dedicated myself to attaining them.

As I achieved one goal, I would feel like the cyclist who by dint of perseverance succeeds in winning a sprint. Finally I lapped the pack—or at least that is the way my superiors viewed it. The triumph, however, was not mine alone, for when the nation's president, Guillermo León Valencia, placed the Cross of Boyacá on my breast, he was symbolically honoring all the noncoms of Colombia.

On April 6, 1965, an Avianca plane was bearing me swiftly to the beautiful capital of the country. On the following day my wife and our daughters, aged three and two, were making a similar trip from Armenia to Bogotá, accompanied by Colonel V.V.

The commandant of the Military Cadet School, an institution founded in 1907 by the illustrious General Reyes, received me in his quarters and was host to my family.

I shall never forget the afternoon of the 7th of April. A timid sun tried to neutralize the late afternoon chill of the savannah. One by one the units of the Brigade of Military Institutes formed a front on the parade grounds: the Military Cadet School in their helmets with golden insignia; the different schools and the delegations of noncoms from the military forces and the police from every garrison in the country. Flags and standards waved their colors in the breeze as bands, military and marching, made the environs shake in their harmony.

Then, honors to the president, who occupied the principal box in company with the minister of war, the commanders of the armed services, and the brigade commander. Loudspeakers filled the wide expanse with the voice of the reader of the citation. As the "whereas's" boomed forth my heart beat rapidly at this supreme moment of my professional life.

Months before, I had been separated from my companions, lost in the Andean brush, having infiltrated a band of criminals, with whom I lived in order to study them and destroy them.

Now I was sharing in a solemn ceremony with my comrades and I was receiving the approving looks of the reader of the citation, of the generals of the republic, and of the military attachés.

At attention, my hands at my sides and my head erect, I stared over the crowded reviewing stand at a stretch of blue sky that extended to the horizon. I knew that a few yards away my wife and daughters watched me proudly and tenderly. While the president was fastening the decoration on my olive-green uniform, to the accompaniment of blaring trumpets and the roll of drums, I was thinking of the treasures laid up for my children, treasures more valuable than all the platinum of Chocó, more valuable than all the gold the State Bank could collect in its depositories: the honor of being a noncom decorated with the Cross of Boyacá!

59 · Commentary

The experience acquired by our military forces in the struggle against the antisocial elements—be they called *guerrilleros, bandoleros,* kidnappers, or robbers—puts us in the vanguard in South America in the matter of counterrevolutionary warfare.

The purpose of this book has not been to examine the origins of *la violencia* or the causes that nourish it. Rather, this book is merely a sincere, dispassionate, chronological account of episodes lived by an Army noncom during a period of difficulty—but a difficulty now overcome, fortunately for the welfare of Colombia.

It is better to receive experience condensed in books or lectures than to have to live it oneself; so I will feel well rewarded for my modest services to our country if the reading of the preceding chapters redounds to the benefit of my comrades in arms.

There is no book, however useless it may seem, from which one cannot learn a lesson. This statement, from Pliny, encouraged me to write these memoirs, in which, also, many Colombian soldiers will be able to behold themselves as in a mirror—soldiers who, during fifteen years of fighting in different regions affected by *la violencia,* have carried out operations similar to, or more beneficial than, the ones I have described. (I have omitted some episodes that are similar to the ones included in order not to extend the work too much and tire the reader.)

But I do wish, before ending, to express some opinions on *la violencia* and the military forces, feelings that have no pretension of being "regulations," but which may be of some help to men in service.

I know that some of my statements are already included in instructional manuals for use in our army; others are just modest suggestions derived from my experiences. If I depart from the paths of orthodoxy, I do so to call my companions' attention to the novelty of the idea, and in no way am I trying to set down doctrine.

1. The *Bandolero* Mystique

The force that drives the *bandolero* to carry out all kinds of depradations is easy money, or at least, the desire for the rapid acquisition of money. Political questions are involved in the lust for wealth. Conrado Salazar once told me he already had a hundred and twenty thousand pesos in cash to buy a *finca* in the *llanos* of Casanare.

The chiefs of the *cuadrillas* and their followers have a particular political party, although they may not understand its programs, its doctrines, much less its principles.

There are *cuadrillas* absolutely communist in nature, but in these comments I refer specifically to the *bandolero* that scourged the Quindío in the last six years.

When the *bandolero* reached a region where the inhabitants held political opinions contrary to his own and there was resistance to the payment of extortion money, the *bandolero* killed without pity.

On a few occasions the *bandolero* sacrificed his own comrades, either for ambition or fear or vengeance.

Of course, the beneficiary of any depredation is always communism, which takes advantage of chaos, disorder, and discontent by casting the blame for all that has happened on the government and the system of government.

2. Collaborators

Not all those who are here are collaborators, nor are all who are collaborators here. This well-known statement is applicable to events resulting from *la violencia*. There were citizens who collaborated with the *cuadrillas* to save their lives, or because, living in extreme poverty, they needed to earn a few pesos. "The highest morality crumbles when human well-being crosses the threshold of misery."

Others, genuine collaborators, in the city, helped the gangs; these were cases of wealthy landowners or politicians with some influence out in the rural areas.

Believe it or not, as Ripley would say, there were instances of hacienda owners who paid the *cuadrillas* so the latter, with their men and methods, would look after the interests of the hacienda owner.

And there were politicians who frequented the haunts of the *bandoleros* in order to determine how they could be of service to them.

The motive? Let the sociologists look into that, though in my opinion ambition and fear were the motives behind such outrageous behavior.

In stating what I have said so far, I am not laying the blame on this political party or the other; I am merely generalizing. My superiors are familiar with the information I have reported in this regard, and they know I am telling the truth.

3. Heroism? No! . . . *Bandolerismo!*

The experience gained over ten years of fighting *bandoleros* gives me the oral right to say that the *bandolero* has no redeeming virtues. The *bandoleros* as heroes? No, criminals. When he meets a man who stands up to him, the *bandolero* turns coward and looks for a way to escape.

I admit there are exceptions, but they just prove the rule.

They are brave when their ambush of the troops goes well; then they do not spare their prisoners, even those that are seriously wounded. The *bandolero* never fights hand-to-hand with the army or the police even when he has a temporary superiority in men and equipment.

Let the communiques of the brigade commanders and the newspaper articles confirm or deny this: there are instances of one man alone putting an entire *cuadrilla* to flight.

4. Discipline

There is no overall code of conduct or set of regulations that governs life in the *cuadrillas*. Rather, obedience is blind, under threat of paying with one's life for the least infraction, as can be seen in certain episodes in this book. Remember that the antisocial elements who operate as bands of outlaws have organizations and procedures entirely of their own making.

Whoever joins a *cuadrilla* knows he is staking his life, shooting the works, for it will be very difficult (if not impossible) for him to leave the band—except as a dead man.

To meet the needs of internal administration the leader makes lists, using the aliases, and issues rudimentary orders of the day, which pass from hand to hand for the information of those who know how to read, and for those who do not, as well. For the illiterate there is always someone in the band to translate the hen-scratches.

Massacres, ambushes, attacks on the supply convoys, etc. are not undertaken suddenly. There is issued something like an operations order, and it's too bad for the *bandolero* who makes a mistake in carrying out his assignments in the operation, because in the *cuadrilla* the only known punishment is death.

5. Good Advice

If one of my comrades should happen to ask me for advice about achieving success in this type of irregular warfare, I would tell him straightway:

Keep yourself physically and spiritually strong. Be careful with alcohol. Be careful with gambling. Moderation is the soldier's best protection.

Participate actively and alertly in combat exercises. Make a sport of, and practice diligently in, marksmanship exercises with revolver, rifle, carbine, and pistol. Read the regulations; study constantly, find in books the complement to what you already know. I have already said that there is no book, however useless it may seem, from which one cannot learn something.

In this matter of guerrilla warfare there are books, both foreign and domestic, that should be consulted.

6. In Recognition of My Superiors

I attribute a good part of the effectiveness of my efforts to the confidence my superiors placed in me. I always enjoyed freedom of action, and I never failed to try to merit the confidence they showed.

When the leader knows how to command he finds subordinates who know how to obey. In order to respond to a good commander the subordinates are willing even to make sacrifices, when the situation requires it.

Let this be the opportunity for me to affirm my admiration for Colonel G.G. and Colonel A.A., who commanded the 8th Brigade with singular effectiveness. In this regard let me repeat from the military handbook:

"The ability to command is one of the most positive characteristics a person can have. In civilian life it means success. In military life the meaning is not changed; it means winning battles, carrying out an assignment. The absence of this ability leads to mediocrity in civilian life; in the army it leads to needless sacrifice of human life on the battlefield, and to failure, in peacetime as well as in war."

7. *La violencia* Was Not Invented in Colombia

After sixteen years the *violencia* phenomenon is, to borrow a term used in flying, in a tailspin. We are witnessing its death rattle, its last gasps.

But we Colombians did not invent *la violencia*! When one studies the history of the European countries one sees that each chapter is written with the blood of thousands of human beings, the result of long and exceedingly cruel struggles. In the hecatomb that began in 1914 and ended with the Treaty of Versailles twelve million people died. Scarcely a quarter of a century ago the Second World War resulted in apocalyptic numbers of victims: forty million! The flower of Europe's youth and part of America's disappeared amidst the roar of planes and the explosion of grenades. In Japan atomic bombs destroyed two important cities in a matter of seconds.

If we compare our misfortunes with those of the nations of Europe and Asia we will see that we are, in spite of our woes, a fortunate country! Praise be to God! This does not mean that we ought to be indifferent to the phenomenon of *la violencia*, for we could well apply to ourselves the aphorism: Only fools take comfort in the fact that many others are in dire straits! I mean, rather, that we must not allow ourselves to be overcome by the pessimism of the pusillanimous; we must have faith in the future.

The fact that we have been able to surmount so many difficulties, shows that we have sufficient physical and moral reserves to move forward toward the fulfillment of our historic destiny.

8. An Obligation Shared by all Colombians

To conclude, I should like to leave a "remember this" directed to all my compatriots, who, with the reading of this book, will have an opportunity to appraise the task of pacification performed by the military forces.

Just as the *patria* is not the exclusive patrimony of one institution or of a few combined, so the pacification of the country is not a task reserved solely to the military forces and the police.†

"Subversion of law and order from within in the present circumstances can be as dangerous as an attack on our territory by another nation."

---

†This idea, that Colombia as a nation is responsible for solving the ravages of *la violencia*, rather than merely the armed forces, has been stated by competent observers such as Gonzalo Canal Ramírez (Colombian Ambassador to the Soviet Union, 1970–72). But the academic

If soldier and civilian are united in the praiseworthy aim
of destroying the *bandolero* wherever he manifests himself,
the *bandolero* will cease to be a threat to society. Furthermore, communism, which waits and relies on the *bandolero*
as its best ally, will be thwarted indefinitely.

We Colombians have demonstrated that we are not
inferior to the generation that gave us liberty.

Despite everything, despite our fratricidal wars and our
calamities, we have preserved and will continue to preserve
the sacred treasure that our heroes, through their efforts and
through their martyrdom, have bequeathed to us: Liberty.

60 · Epilogue

On Maundy Thursday of this year, 1965, the jet left me, with
my wife and children, at the Callao International Airport in
Lima. It was ten in the evening when we stepped on Peruvian
soil after a fast two-hour flight from the capital of Colombia.

Having never traveled by jet I was astounded by the speed
as the huge machine hurtled down the runway at Bogotá. But
the ministrations of the stewardess of Avianca, our great air-
line, calmed me completely and without the slightest incident
we reached Peru, once the wealthiest colony of the crown of
Spain.

Now the problem was to find the military attaché, whom

---

literature on this point has been politicized by liberal writers, who cling
to the absurd notion that there would be no *violencia* if there were no
military repression; by Marxists, who oppose all stability organs of non-
Marxist governments; and by conservatives, who blame all social disruptions on communism. Buitrago reflects an understandable bitterness on
this subject.

I knew only by description. It is not very pleasant to find oneself suddenly in a foreign land when one is a novice in these mysteries. So while I was waiting in line to have my passport checked, I looked around, trying to spot in the crowd a gentleman more or less of my height, but bushy-browed—a feature, according to General R.R., that would make it easy for me to recognize Colonel P.

Lima was enjoying the splendor of summer, with a climate warmer than Cali's and Pereira's. At night the avenues were bathed in light from the signs and from the stream of cars that came and went in a never-ending procession. During the day a multitude headed for the nearby beaches to take advantage of the few sunny days left in the warm season; soon the beaches would be deserted until December, because of the cold and the effects of the Humboldt current, or perhaps other reasons.

Through arrangements by the government of my country, and at the suggestion of the high command, I was to be the secretary to the military and air attaché at the Colombian embassy in Lima.

Behind me lay ten years of continual struggle against *bandoleros*. Now, as a reward for the hard fight, I was in a foreign country. At first, of course, since I was no longer confronted by dangerous patrols but rather by typewriters, desks, and stacks of papers, I missed the emotion of combat. But I adjusted to the medium with a facility that surprised me. Before yielding to the restorative repose of the night's sleep or of Lima's traditional siesta, I would find myself thinking back. As in a movie projected within my brain the episodes of my eventful military life flashed on the screen of my mind.

One day I made a resolution: I would write my memoirs. This was the first step; the rest followed naturally.

Everything was not a bed of roses in this "golden exile," as these assignments out of the country are often called. I received phone calls, threats, and intimidations, and one morning when I got up I found in front of my door an anonymous note that read:

Reports to superiors, detective escort, visits to the prefect of
Lima and to the Intelligence Service of the Peruvian Army.

Just as you did with our comrades . . .

So *bandolerismo* had ramifications that reached into
Peru? Then it was neither fancy nor fiction, that business
about the hand of communism being behind some *cuadrillas*
of *bandoleros* in Colombia.

In June appeared the first signs of *bandoleros* in the
Peruvian sierra. Even when it was being roundly declared that
this was a question of simple cattle rustlers, the government,
the congress, and the military forces all admitted the existence of spots of subversive activity, "of seditious elements
who wished to distrupt public order in order to impose the
communistic system."

Pecutá, Mesa Pelada, Santa Rosa, Andamarca, Yahuarima,
Satipo, Juan de la Puente Uceda, etc.

Several policemen killed in ambush, troop movements,
military flights; the death penalty for traitors, etc. But withal
a great solidarity between governing and governed, working
together to exorcise the evil—a solidarity that does credit to
the Peruvian people.†

On official business, I traveled to La Paz. There I witnessed the May revolution in which there occurred clashes
between workers and the military forces that left a residue of
over a hundred dead. Had it not been for the *soroche*,* which

---

†While Buitrago loyally commends the Peruvians on the putting down
of domestic communist guerrillas in 1965, the situation was not at all
comparable to what happened earlier in Colombia. This fact was proved
just a few months later when the Peruvian military forces suspended
civilian political processes in the name of preempting leftist revolutionary action and carried out some strong reforms of their own.
Furthermore, Peru never had the *bandoleroismo* as Colombia did, and
the brief 1965 Peruvian uprising was a totally unsuccessful attempt by
intellectual leftists of white European extraction to communize traditional Indian communities.

*Illness experienced at high altitudes. Mailaise that one feels on climb-

laid me low, sending me to bed for ten days, I would have enjoyed my visit in the capital of Bolivia, that very high city surrounded by snow-capped peaks whose tips touched the sky.

The sight of the Illimani massif in the fiery sunsets evoked memories of my expeditions with the troops of the 6th and 8th Brigades, along the slopes of the Nevado de Tolima, and little by little I was filling pages with accounts of the episodes of *la violencia* that it had been my lot to experience. How many soldiers sacrificed! How many unknown heroes who gave themselves for their country!

Over the surface of Lake Titicaca I sailed, driven by the stiff breeze that filled the sails. As I contemplated the intense blue that extended beyond my vision, I was remembering my hours of anguish and anxiety spent in the *cuadrilla* of Conrado with Tista and Gata.

Back in Lima I added details to the account and put in order the chapters that today I submit to my superiors, to my comrades, and to my countrymen.

The Bogotá papers have carried an extensive chronicle of the *bandoleros* over the past year. Harold Eder, a wealthy industrialist from Valle del Cauca, was killed by the *cuadrilla* of Tijeras, a *bandolero* who months later was felled by the bullets of the law. Oliverio Lara Borrero was kidnapped on the same land his efforts had made prosperous. As in the novel by Rivera, there was "no trace of him; the jungle swallowed him up." Efraín González, the terror of Santander and Boyacá, a companion of mine in the military-police battalion before he decided to follow a life of crime, fell to the relentless pursuit of the army, in downtown Bogotá.†

---

ing at great height above sea level. The troops of the Liberator, Simón Bolívar, had to deal with *soroche* when they crossed the gigantic barrier of the Andes in order to reach the *pampa* of Junín in 1824.

†Buitrago is describing here the end of *la violencia*. Eder's kidnappers were a pro-Castro gang that was wiped out with surgical precision. Efraín González was shot down in a Bogotá housing project after several soldiers were killed and more wounded while trying to capture him alive.

In the land of Francisco Pizarro, spring is being announced officially, but the sun still is covered by a heavy layer of clouds and the *garrúa*, sad and ever-present, prolongs the winter over the homeland of Santa Rosa and San Martín de Porres.

Lima, Peru
October, 1965

POSTSCRIPT

It is June 22, 1967. I have just arrived at the town of Granada, Meta. I have the task of identifying the body of a *bandolero* slain in combat with the army.

It is raining hard and a muddy expanse surrounds us. I am with the B-2, the intelligence officer, of the Villavicencio Brigade on the way to the hospital, or what passes for such there.

"Do you recognize this pistol?"

"Yes, Major! I saw it in the possession of David Salazar, alias Gladis, Zarpazo's brother, when we were in the *cuadrilla*. You've got a big fish here!"

I do not have to enter the hospital. From outside I recognize the bodies, which are already in a state of decomposition through the effects of time and weather. Here is Zarpazo, the man who filled the rich regions of Colombia with blood and terror.† Cursed be his name and cursed be those who helped him in his crime and destruction!

For a few minutes I question the concubine of the dead *bandolero*. She recognizes me! She is trembling; she is terrified; she is wounded in both legs. She is crying. She is pregnant.

Oh, Lord, how mysterious are thy ways!

---

†Zarpazo had moved his base of operations from the Cauca Valley to the eastern plains, where the geography and local culture are very different. Thanks to the open terrain and to effective civic-assistance programs there, *la violencia* was easily controlled after 1953, and Zarpazo was one of several flashy *bandoleros* who fell quickly after relocating in this part of Colombia.

144 Colombianos Murieron Asesinados por "Zarpazo"

Cali, 21. — "Con la muerte de Conrado Salazar (a. Zarpazo), ocurrida hoy en el Meta, a manos de las fuerzas del orden, desaparece uno de los más siniestros personajes y se cierra uno de los capítulos más sombríos de la violencia en el Valle", dijo esta tarde, en declaraciones para El Tiempo, el abogado Marino Escobar Ayala, jefe de orden público del Valle. quien agregó que el antisocial abatido estaba sindicado de no menos de 100 muertes violentas, por acciones directas o indirectas.

El "récord" criminal

Conrado Salazar, quien también era conocido con el remoquete de "Don Salas", había nacido en Obando (Valle) y tenía en la actualidad unos 34 años de edad, hijo de los esposos Bautista Salazar y Julia García de Salazar. Era de baja estatura pero fornido, cabello liso, ojos negros y tez morena conse...

Estaba condenado a cuatro siglos de presidio, en caso de haber sido capturado.—Siete genocidios catalogados como ignominiosos, perpetró en los departamentos del Valle del Cauca, Quindío y Risaralda.—Una pesadilla histórica conforman sus antecedentes.

operaban especialmente en las zonas montañosas de Obando, Toro, Alcalá, Cartago y zonas circunvecinas. Dicha cuadrilla tenía conexiones con la de "Puente Roto", otro jefe bandolero que operaba especialmente en regiones de Sevilla y Calcedonia, muerto también en acción contra el ejército.

Gobernador en peligro

El primer lugar.teniente de "Zarpazo" era el bandolero Tista Tabares, igualmente muerto ya, autor de un frustrado asalto en 1964 a una comisión de altos funcionarios, encabezados por

Boletín informativo de orden público Nº 013:

El Comando del Ejército hace saber que en desarrollo de informes recibidos sobre la presencia del bandolero Conrado Salazar García (a. Zarpazo) en la región de San Juan de Arama (departamento del Meta) tropas

"Zarpazo" Muerto por el Ejército

Villavicencio, 21. — Una patrulla del Batallón Vargas dio de baja a la madrugada de hoy al bandolero José Milciades Cortés o Julio Conrado Salazar García, uno de los criminales que durante mu-

crodactilias y enviarlas a Bogotá para los efectos de la plena identificación técnica.

El coronel Alvaro Ovalle Paz. comandante de la VII Brigada, expidió el boletín informativo número 1, en el cual da cuen-

The translator, M. Murray Lasley, is Associate Professor of Spanish at the University of Florida, Gainesville, Florida.

The editor and annotator, Russell W. Ramsey, is Principal, Alternative School, Alachua County Public Schools, Gainesville, Florida.

ZARPAZO THE BANDIT
was composed in IBM Press Roman by
The Blue Ridge Group, Ltd., East Flat Rock, N.C.,
printed by McNaughton-Gunn, Inc., Ann Arbor, Michigan,
and bound by Kingsport Press, Kingsport, Tennessee.
Editor: Francis P. Squibb
Production: Paul R. Kennedy
Book and jacket design: Anna F. Jacobs